# THE CHOSEN TWELVE PLUS ONE

# THE CHOSEN TWELVE PLUS ONE

Portraits by Harry A. Hollett
Text by Clarence E. Macartney

MULTNOMAH PRESS
PORTLAND, OREGON 97266

# Preface

It is a rare moment when two art forms so complement one another that, in effect, they become one in style and in purpose.

This has happened in the creation of The Chosen Twelve Plus One. The portrait masterpieces of Harry A. Hollett and the literary talents of Clarence Edward Noble Macartney have been blended in the pages of this book to produce a volume unparalleled in its scope and excellence.

Hollett, a nationally acclaimed and award-winning portrait photographer, took fifteen years to select his models for the apostles and complete the portrait project. Macartney, a gifted writer and minister of the first half of this century, originally gathered these literary sketches of the apostles into one of the forty-seven volumes which he authored.

Both the portraits and the prose bring into the reader's focus the lives of the founders of Christianity. And ultimately, even though Jesus Christ is not portrayed in this book, the reader's attention will be centered on the One Who is the entire foundation for the Christian faith.

Here then, for your approval, is The Chosen Twelve Plus One.

The Publisher

Text adapted from *Of Them He Chose Twelve* by Clarence Macartney.

Unless otherwise indicated, all Scripture quotations are from *The King James Version*.

Scripture quotations marked RV are from *The English Revised Version*.

THE CHOSEN TWELVE PLUS ONE
©1980 by Multnomah Press
Portland, Oregon

First printing 1980
Printed in the United States of America

**Library of Congress Cataloging in Publication Data**

Hollett, Harry, 1911-
    The chosen twelve plus one.

    "Text adapted from Of them He chose twelve,
by Clarence Macartney."
    1. Photography—Portraits.  2. Apostles—
Iconography.  3. Apostles.  I. Macartney, Clarence
Edward Noble, 1879-1957.  II. Macartney, Clarence
Edward Noble, 1879-1957. Of them He chose twelve.
III. Title.
TR680.H64      779'.862      80-17881

ISBN 0-930014-43-X

# Contents

# An Introduction to the Portraits

This magnificent collection of photographs, conceived and executed by Harry A. Hollett, a photographer for more than 50 years, can and should be enjoyed by each viewer on several different levels.

The spiritual experience must be considered first. Harry Hollett is a devout man who has received Christ as his personal Lord and Saviour. Anyone looking at this collection quite likely will agree that Harry has given us a unique conceptualization of those who were the early associates of Christ.

As you look at these men, I hope that you too will feel drawn closer to the one whom they acknowledged as their Lord and Master—Jesus Christ.

A second level of enjoyment of these portraits is the artistic level. Examine each one as a work of art. The composition of each is different, yet, while complete in itself, each portrait complements all the others. The colors are most appropriate to the faces and the backgrounds. The total group seems to be a total experience, yet the viewer is inescapably brought to the realization of the one who is not shown—the leader, the transcendent and redeeming Christ. These are indeed great works of art.

A third level of enjoyment is the technical proficiency shown by the photographer. Note the different poses of the various models. Observe the focus, here razor sharp, there diffused, whatever will enhance the mood of the picture. Notice the lighting—also matched to the mood, to the pose, to the background of the apostle portrayed, and to the colors used. Truly Harry Hollett is a master of his craft.

A fourth level of enjoyment is a study of the faces Harry selected to be his models. Most of them are strong faces showing great character and idealism. The brooding, heartbroken Judas provides a sharp contrast to the stalwart Peter, the skeptical Thomas, and the methodical Matthew. Look carefully at the face of Paul. Though denied the personal ex-

*perience of the original Twelve, he saw the future even more clearly than they, and this is reflected in his face. The selection of these models was superb.*

*However, the technical skill, the artistic portraiture, the superb selection of models, and even the general acceptance of this collection by the public does not really define the collection. A guiding presence accompanied each step of the production. Harry and I know who it was. We hope you do, too.*

*Paul M. Morrill*
*Sun City, Arizona*

# An Introduction to the Text

*A number of years ago I purchased from an unfortunate art dealer a copy of Leonardo da Vinci's Last Supper. It was more compassion for the broken and aged dealer than love for this kind of art that moved me to make the purchase, although I had every reason to accept the high judgment which he passed on the picture. When I had secured the picture it became a problem of disposition, rather than a subject for admiration, its dimensions rendering it out of place in any ordinary room or study. At length I shipped it to my old home in Pennsylvania and hung it on the wall of the dining-room.*

*During a long stay at home one summer, I frequently examined the painting and began to appreciate for the first time its great excellence and to understand how this work of da Vinci's became so famous. A casual and occasional glance let me see just twelve men of flowing robes and Hebraic cast of countenance sitting at table with their Master. But continued and repeated observation began to reveal more than a mere group of thirteen men, very much alike. I began to see the individuality, the personality of each member of the group: the clutching avarice of Judas, the dreamy mysticism of Bartholomew, the burning zeal of Simon, the impulsive aggressiveness of Peter and the despairing melancholy of Thomas.*

*Our general and occasional reading of the New Testament may be likened to a careless glance at the Italian's masterpiece, for we see a number of men and do not mark much difference between them. The careful study of the New Testament reveals more than that; it rewards us by making each one of the Twelve Disciples stand out in his own personality and individuality. It is indeed true that of some of the disciples we know hardly anything, but even when their name in a catalogue of the Twelve is all that we have to go by, it is possible to frame a distinct conception of each of the Twelve men chosen by Christ to build the church upon the foundation which He Himself had laid.*

*In one of his essays, William Hazlitt speaks of Charles Lamb and some of his friends discussing the question of persons they would like to have known. Lamb dismisses Sir Isaac Newton and William Locke, stars of the first magnitude, because, although distinguished and notable for their achievements, they were not characters, not real persons. "Yes, the greatest names, but they were not persons, not persons." This study of the Twelve Disciples shall not have been in vain if it shall result in taking these twelve men out from their hiding-place between the covers of the Bible and making them live before us as interesting and, in the Providence of God, mighty personalities, humble and unlearned, it is true; but nevertheless human forces acting at the sources of Christian history and, therefore, mighty agents of destiny.*

*But there are reasons other than those of mere curiosity or biographical interest. The four men who wrote the Gospels bearing their names were not, it is to be remembered, writing biographical sketches of the disciples of Christ. The Great Personality about whom they are thinking and writing is Christ. Whatever they tell us of Peter, John, Andrew, and the rest, is but incidental to the story of the Son Himself about whom these lesser lights cluster. It is the study of these men that compels us to study the Master who had chosen them out of the world to witness for Him before men.*

*We cannot earnestly and prayerfully study the lives and characters of the Twelve Apostles without coming to a better understanding of the mission, and a clearer vision of the glorious character of Him who spent most of the time of His ministry upon earth in training the Twelve by precept, by example, by love and patience, by warning and rebuke, by miracle and by daily companionship. Despite temptations and temporary lapses, the disciples, as a body, remained true to Christ and the work He had given them to do. This magnificent fidelity was based upon complete confidence in the Person of Jesus, and that confidence was possible only because of their intimacy with Him. If we know the Apostles better we shall be rewarded by knowing better Him, whom to know aright is Eternal Life. In the words of one of the chief students in this fascinating field, the author of* The Training of the Twelve,

*"All, therefore, who desire to get the benefit of this trust, must be willing to spend time and take the trouble to get into the heart of the Gospel story, and of its great subject. The sure anchorage is not attainable by a listless, random reading of the evangelistic narratives, but by a close, careful, prayerful study, pursued, it may be, for years. Those who grudge the trouble are in imminent danger of the fate which befell the ignorant multitude, being liable to be thrown into panic by every new infidel book, or to be scandalized by every strange utterance of the object of faith. Those, on the other hand, who do take the trouble, will be rewarded for their pains. Storm-tossed for a time, they shall at length reach the harbor of creed which is no nondescript compromise between infidelity and Scriptural*

Christianity, but embraces all the cardinal facts and truths of the faith as taught by Jesus."

In John's great vision of the holy city, the New Jerusalem, which had the glory of God, he tells us that the twelve gates of the city were inscribed with the names of the twelve tribes of Israel, but that the twelve foundations of the city were engraved with the twelve names of the Apostles of the Lamb. If the names of the twelve tribes of Israel on the gates of the city suggest the completeness of the company of the saved and the fulness of redemption, the names of the Twelve Apostles of the Lamb graven on the twelve foundations remind us that upon the foundation which they laid in Jesus Christ was builded the whole vast structure of Christian history. Therefore it is that their names live forever.

# THE CHOSEN
# TWELVE
# PLUS ONE

# ANDREW

With the mention of Andrew begins the long day of Christian history. Obscure are the beginnings of nations and systems and men. Not less so were the beginnings of the Christian Church.

John was beyond Jordan baptizing. It was the second day after he had baptized Jesus. John and two of his disciples were standing by the roadside when Jesus passed by. As He passed, John exclaimed, "Behold the Lamb of God!" One of the two disciples was Andrew (John 1:40), and he with his companion, in all probability John, having heard what John the Baptist had said about Jesus, turned to follow Him.

With that turning begins Christian history, Christian discipleship. What if Andrew and his companion had not turned! That act on their part was like a pebble on yonder mountain ridge which obstructs the rain that has fallen and turns it to the east or to the west, to the north or to the south. So from the heights of will and desire, the will and the desire of Andrew and his unnamed but not unknown companion, descended the stream of Christian history.

Andrew's antecedents are good. He appears first in the sacred narrative as a disciple of John the Baptist. That meant that he appreciated spiritual values, that the mighty proclamation of the Baptist about repentance and judgment and the Kingdom of God found response in his fisherman's heart. The synoptical evangelists make no mention of the first meeting between Christ and the men who were to become His disciples. But John treasures it among his most sacred memories, and after the sublime introduction to his Gospel he relates that casual, apparently insignificant meeting when Andrew and he turned to follow One whom they had heard the Baptist describe as the Lamb of God.

They that seek ever find. Jesus, seeing them following, knowing all that was in their hearts, said to them, "What seek ye?" They said unto Him, "Master, where dwellest Thou?" He said unto them, "Come and see." They came and saw where He dwelt, and abode with Him that day; for it was about the tenth hour. What they talked about during that visit we know not. "Something sealed the lips of that evangelist." But the result was that Andrew, at least, went away convinced that Jesus was the Messiah, the Christ.

On our dull ears today that announcement falls like a commonplace. It awakens, alas, no thrill of hope or expectation. But with Andrew it was different. The devout Hebrew knew the voices and signs and promises of the past about Israel's coming Redeemer, the Prince of Peace, the Mighty Counselor, the Dayspring from on high, the Desire of the nations, the Star out of Jacob, and the Sceptre out of Israel. A few hours in the company of a strange young man on the other side Jordan, and Andrew was convinced that Jesus was Christ.

Millions have believed on Jesus as the Christ, the Son of God, the Saviour of the world. What a host as they pass by in review, called out of every nation and tribe and kindred and people and tongue, out of every age —the men, the women, the little children! They have believed in Jesus and have worshipped Him and prayed to Him as Christ. At the head of that glorious procession comes Andrew, the first fruits of the world, his lips the first to frame the accents of faith, his confession the first note in that chorus which is to grow in volume from age to age and which this day makes heaven and earth ring with its Te Deum of praise —"Thou art the everlasting Son of the Father, O Christ!"

It meant so much to Andrew, this discovery about Jesus, that he must share it with someone else. With whom? With his own brother, Simon. "He first findeth his own brother Simon, and saith unto him, We have found the Messiah, the Christ. And he brought him to Jesus." Incomparable indeed is this scene of the beginning of Christianity — Andrew bringing Peter his brother to Jesus! Andrew was not only the first believer, he was the first Christian worker. To him it fell to speak the first good word for Jesus Christ, to bring the first man to Jesus. He is the forerunner of all those who have told men of Christ and have brought others to His feet. For that reason, if there are ranks and distinctions in heaven, I think that not only will the Twelve Apostles seated upon thrones be marked in heaven for their great service to Christ, but Andrew will have about him a peculiar halo as the man who first believed in Christ and brought the first man unto Him.

It said much for the family relationship that it was his own brother that Andrew went to first of all with the news of the Messiah. It is not difficult to think of families where a man would tell anyone else before he would tell his own brother; sometimes because of animosities and quarreling which make it impossible, even when the heart is full and the mind is earnest; sometimes because of a strange and yet natural hesitancy to speak on these subjects to our own flesh and blood.

"But do speak with him; I feel that a stranger will have more influence with him than one of his own family." How often is that word spoken to minister or religious worker! It is not normal; it is not the way in which Christianity began to spread in the world. It began to spread by one brother telling another about Christ. It may be that your word for Christ, for God, for the eternal things, spoken to your own flesh and blood, those so near to you that they never expect you to mention the matter to them, will prove to be the word "spoken in season," seed sown upon good soil.

We hear very little of Andrew after this; on two other occasions only (John 6:1-14; Mark 13:3). But there is no need to tell us anything else. Whatever Andrew may have done during the years with Jesus, or whatever signs and wonders he may have wrought when the power of the Holy Ghost descended upon him at Pentecost, he never did a greater work than when he brought Peter to Christ. Peter is Andrew's claim to greatness. You ask me, What did Andrew do? The answer is, Peter. Men not otherwise noted, plain, steady-going, earnest men, have as a rule been the men who have brought great workers for Christ and the Church into the fold.

On a dull winter's day a poor preacher in a London chapel seems to be talking, not to the dozen or so listless hearers on the benches of his chapel, but to a discouraged, perplexed-looking boy on the back seat. The boy was Charles Haddon Spurgeon, later to become one of the great preachers of the faith. Here was his Andrew who brought him to Christ. Andrew was always bringing someone to Jesus. He brought his brother, Peter; he brought the lad with the barley loaves and the two fishes; he brought the enquiring Greeks.

Too few are the Andrews in our midst, in all churches, in the church which we call our home. Christianity cannot grow or flourish or endure or propagate itself because its adherents are able and willing to sing it praises, to defend logically its principles, to live faithfully its precepts, or to state learnedly and eloquently its truths. Nor did it grow and flourish that way. It grew and expanded and influenced the lives of men and nations because it had within its communion men and women who, like Andrew, brought someone else.

To do this, men must appreciate the true greatness and honor of it, and have it as their heart's verdict that the greatest privilege on earth is to be used of God in bringing unto Him to be reconciled one of His own erring children. "They that be wise shall shine as the brightness of the firmament; and they that turn many to righteousness as the stars for ever and ever" (Daniel 12:3). Shine on, faithful Andrew, first to bring a soul to Christ, and let thy spirit fall upon us!

# PETER

They were all human, these men whom Jesus called to follow Him; but Peter reveals more of himself than any of the others, and the self that he shows is so remarkably like the self that followers of Jesus today see in themselves that I venture to name Peter the most human of the Apostles.

We know far more about Peter, both in the Gospels and out of them, than we do of any other disciple. He speaks more frequently than the others and is spoken to frequently by Jesus; the story of the spread of the Church as told in the book of the Acts tells more about what Peter did and said and suffered and where he went than it does about any of the Twelve, or any of the followers of Jesus, save that one whose name and whose deeds were destined to eclipse those of Peter himself.

Not only is Peter the speaker and the actor whom we know best, but when he does speak and act he does so in a manner that is peculiarly self-revelatory. You know persons who speak and act before you, but neither their words nor their actions tell you much about them, the manner of soul that lies beneath that exterior; they are neutral in their conduct, so far as revealing self is concerned. Then there are others who speak and act, but their words and their deeds may be such as give an altogether wrong impression as to their character, deceiving rather than enlightening.

But Peter is one of those whole-hearted men who do whatever they do, in good or in evil, with their whole might, leaving no slightest doubt as to the kind of person who is speaking or acting. Peter could not have hidden his real self or disguised himself had he tried to do it. He was a non-deliberative, warm-hearted, impulsive, quick-acting soul who was mastered by the motive of the moment, whether it was good or bad. Someone has said that the worst disease of the heart is cold. Peter never had that disease, although he had many other sicknesses of the soul.

Take any group of men like these twelve and you will find represented there the types of mankind. Even in a family where there are six or eight, or even four brothers, you will find one who is on the order of Thomas, perhaps, another on the order of James, another who is like Nathanael or like John, and almost always one who is like Peter. In my own family, one of four sons, I had a brother who reminds me of Peter. He was impulsive, affectionate, ready in speech, completely carried away by the enthusiasm of a moment, sometimes boastful as to future accomplishments, sanguine often to the verge of folly, but strong-hearted and strong-minded, awakening in others reciprocal affection and enthusiasm. He had not the balance of another brother, nor the patience of a second, nor the penetration of a third; but these Petrine qualities he possessed to a marked degree. I mention this only to show that it is not difficult to get the measure of Peter. He is one of those men whom we get to know quickly, but who are, notwithstanding, supremely worth knowing.

Even if the Gospels had told us much more about John and James and the others than they do, and yet told us what they have about Peter, I am sure that Peter would be the one we should know the best. His acts and speeches are such as impress themselves upon the mind.

He commences his intercourse with Jesus, at least at the time of the formal call to become a disciple, by falling at the feet of Jesus in the fishing boat and beseeching Him to depart from him, and ends that earthly intercourse with an impulsive and wholly disinterested question about the future of John.

He is the disciple who tries to walk to Jesus on the stormy deep, who would stay with Jesus on the mount of Transfiguration, who will not have Jesus wash his feet, who boasts of his loyalty and then with an oath affirms his disloyalty, who out with a sword and cuts off the ear of Malchus, who brushes aside the hesitating John and goes boldly into the sepulchre, who, when he knows that Jesus is standing on the shore, wraps his fisher's coat about him and plunges into the sea and swims to the shore, unable to wait for the clumsy boats to bring him to Jesus. What a series of striking utterances — dramatic actions!

That leap of his into the sea to get to Christ at once is one of the best of commentaries on the character of Peter. There you have Peter at his best — his redeemed self, full of vigor, full of love, full of action, impulsive, daring, overwhelming you with his glad enthusiasm. It was John who first saw Jesus through the dim mists of the morning. His was the intuitive soul that could apprehend the truth of the sayings of Jesus and grasp the place that Christ had in the mystery of redemption; but it was Peter who hurled himself into the sea.

A character like Peter's cannot be assumed or counterfeited. Nathanael or John would look very foolish if they tried to act like Peter. This leaping activity of soul and body, this effervescence of spirit must be natural. When it is natural it is admired; when assumed it is laughed at.

The mental and physical activity of Peter turns one's mind to the mystery of influence and leadership. It was to this disciple, one who acted and spoke as Peter did, that Jesus gave the leadership; Peter certainly, both in the Gospels and in the Acts, is the leader among the disciples of Jesus. Mere physical alertness and activity have their influence upon the mind of man, and men seem to take naturally to the leadership of those who do not wait for the appointment of leadership, but assume it.

Apart, then, from his spiritual endowments and the training which he received from Jesus, Peter had those native physical qualities which are magnetic and draw men to him who possesses them. It is indeed a great gift, but woe to him who tries to put on even a physical alertness and enthusiasm which is not native to him. But the genuine thing as Peter possessed it is one of the foundations of true leadership.

Jesus Himself told this Apostle, "Thou art Peter, and upon this rock I will build My Church, and the gates of hell shall not prevail against it." There is a naturalness in this elevation of Peter, because Christianity claims to be a universal religion and as such must be adapted to men of every kind of mind and disposition. Peter, more than any of the Apostles, is representative of the universal man.

Paul was the chosen Apostle to the Gentiles, yet magnificently gifted as he was, he represents a special type, the devotee, the scholar, the philosopher. So does John the mystic, so does Bartholomew the dreamer. Peter was not an average, two-talent man by any means, but he certainly represents humanity in its length and breadth and depth and height more than any other Apostle. He was not too dull, nor was he too gifted, not stupid, nor yet too profound.

These traits come out in his two Letters, which are wonderfully self-revealing. Indeed, if one were asked to select out of the New Testament a series of passages best adapted for the guidance of the average Christian in all parts of the world, in all ages of man, one could not do better than make a little volume out of the sayings of Peter. One would omit, of course, his references to the ark and to Christ preaching to the dead and much of his eschatological thunderings, not because they have not their place, but because one is looking for passages which at once will direct and guide the Christian believer. With the exception of these few portions, where in the Bible could one secure such a manual for everyday Christian experience? There is a fitness, then, in this elevation of Peter to a place of representative authority. Take him all in all, he is the best model and the best teacher for men at large.

Peter had a wife, and we cannot but wonder what kind of wife she was. She must have been a credit and a help to him, else he had not carried her about with him on his missionary tours as we are told by Paul he did. It had been sad indeed had that splendid enthusiast been compelled to go about with a cold millstone of a wife hung about his eager neck, mocking at his zeal and pointing out his inconsistencies, of which there were probably not a few. We infer, both from this fact that his wife went about with him, and also from the reading of his two Letters, that she was a real benediction to him, for no New Testament writer touches with such adornment the subject of marriage and the duties of husbands towards their wives and of wives towards their husbands.

Paul indeed makes Christ's love for the Church the symbol of the love that men ought to bear to their wives, and a great and moving passage it is; nevertheless, we cannot forget, at least some cannot, that it is Paul who conceives of woman's place in a negative more than a positive sense, dwelling upon what woman is not to do rather than upon what she may do.

But it is Peter who makes that tender and lovely, though oft abused, reference to woman as the "weaker vessel" to whom honor is due. What eloquent sermons have been preached upon that text! —preached, not merely in the pulpit, but in the burning house out of which first the woman is carried, in the horrid areas of war and invasion; written, too, on the decks of the doomed *Titanic,* or the sinking *Lusitania,* when strong men stood back from the boats and did immortal honor to the weaker vessel of womanhood and childhood.

From the beginning to the end of his career, as it is sketched for us in the Gospels, Peter is "consistently inconsistent." He hails Jesus as the Son of God and the next moment tries to dissuade Him from His redemptive work, bringing upon himself the rebuke, "Get thee behind Me, Satan!" He believed that Jesus could support him on the swelling waves of Galilee, but his faith forsook him when he found himself beyond the safety of the boat. He protests against Jesus washing his feet and then wants Him to wash not his feet only, but also his hands and head. He boasted that though all should forsake Jesus, he would be found faithful, and then he denied Him. He cut off the ear of Malchus in the Garden and then forsook Jesus. After his vision on the roof of Simon the tanner, he cast off his Jewish prejudices, but after fraternizing with the Gentile converts at Antioch, withdrew from their company when "certain from James" came down, fearing the censure of that pillar of the Church and his influential party.

Despite these inconsistencies, Peter holds our affection and our admiration. He deserved the stinging and humiliating rebuke administered to him by Paul at Antioch for refusing to associate with the Gentile Christians, and we cannot think of Paul so acting. Nevertheless, Peter is so transparent in his character, so absolute in his actions both for good and for evil, that we never lose interest in him, and his very inconsistencies commend him to us; for if we take the measure of our Christian life, most of us will find that we fall into the class represented by Peter rather than into that represented by the superior and magnificent Paul.

Think how Peter acted at times in ways that were inconsistent with the weakness, the fear, the cowardice that was in him; he thrills us with the possibilities of life—your life and my life. There is no doubt about the elements of weakness within us, but a life like Peter's tells us that it need not always be so with us, that it is possible to rise above this weaker and worse self into the high powers of another and nobler but not less real self. When Peter goes wrong, he always comes back to the right; when he falls, he rises again. Although he often goes wrong, he never impresses you as the sort of man who is content to do evil or who despairs of doing good.

Have you failed? Have you been so weak that it has cost you shame and bitter tears? Have you done evil when you were planning how you would do good? If so, show by your conduct in the future that you can be noble, inconsistent with that past record, and make your solemn vow that the Christ-inspired and Christ-governed better self that is in you will be seen in action and heard in speech and felt in influence.

> Not in their brightness, but their earthly stain
> Are the true seed vouchsafed to earthly eyes,
> And saints are lowered that the world may rise.

No incident in Christian history has been such a source of comfort and warning as the fall of Peter. There is no scene in Scripture which so illustrates the weakness of the human heart and our proneness to sin, and at the same time nothing in the Scriptures or in Christian history which manifests so exquisitely the tender, seeking, restoring love of Jesus Christ. Here is all the pathos of sin —man's denial and rejection of the Son of God. Not since our first parents wept at the gates of Eden had such tears been shed as those which coursed down the fisherman's face when he went out into the night after he had heard the cock crow. We are not angry with Peter, nor indeed greatly amazed at his fall. Our first and last feeling is one of sadness.

There are writers who can make one weep as they recite the wrongs and the sufferings of mankind; and others who can make one weep with the lover or maid upon whom the tragedy of life has fallen. But the Bible makes man weep over sin. Sin is tragic, terrible, but it is also unutterably sad, pathetic. If you would get an understanding of the pathos of sin, behold the look in the face of Jesus as He turns to look upon Peter when he had denied Him for the third time.

Judas was in despair because of his horror at the stature of the evil one that was in him; Peter was in tears because he realized that the worst and weaker Peter had denied Jesus when all the time the better and stronger Peter, his own best self, had been ready and willing to confess Jesus. His was the sorrow not of a man who had done evil that he had planned and then found his mistake, but the sorrow of a man who had done the very thing he hated and left undone the good he would have done.

In the *Tale of Two Cities* Charles Dickens, in describing the grief of the dissipated but gifted lawyer's clerk, tells of the sorrow that man feels when he has been disloyal to himself, and, like Saul, has cast away his shield as if it had not been anointed with oil.

When his host followed him out on the staircase with a candle, to light him down the stairs, the day was coldly looking in through its grimy windows. When he got out of the house, the air was cold and sad, the dull sky overcast, the river dark and dim, the whole scene like a lifeless desert. And wreaths of dust were spinning round and round before the morning blast, as if the desert sand had risen far away, and the first spray of it in its advance had begun to overwhelm the city. Waste forces within him, and a desert all around, this man stood still on his way across a silent terrace, and saw for a moment, lying in the wilderness before him, a mirage of honorable ambition, self-denial and perseverance. In the fair city of this vision there were airy galleries from which the loves and graces looked upon him, gardens in which the fruits of life hung ripening, waters of Hope that sparkled in his sight. A moment, and it was gone. Climbing to a high chamber in a well of houses, he threw himself down in his clothes on a neglected bed, and its pillow was wet with wasted tears. Sadly, sadly, the sun rose; it rose upon no sadder sight than the man of good abilities and good emotions, incapable of their directed exercise, incapable of his own help and his own happiness, sensible of the blight on him, and resigning himself to let it eat him away.

Between the Peter whom we last see going out into the night to weep his bitter tears and the bold death-scorning Apostle of the New Testament, there stands one mighty transforming fact: the resurrection appearance of Jesus to Peter. The angel at the tomb had indeed sent a special message for Peter. "Go, tell His disciples *and Peter*" (Mark 16:7). It was as if the sin of Peter had cast him out of the band of the disciples and that none would think of him as being included in a general message for the disciples.

But more precious than this message was that appearance. It was too sacred for even the Sacred Page. Something sealed the lips of the evangelists, and Peter himself, usually so outspoken and frank in all that happened to him, has not a word to say of it in his two letters. The scene that is painted by the master hand of St. John in the last two pages of his Gospel, the interview between Jesus and Peter by the seashore, was not the restoration of Peter to the Apostolate. It was but a public record or sanction of what had already taken place when Jesus met Peter, and met him alone. We can imagine what Peter said, or rather what Jesus said, for I think this must have been the one time when impetuous, impulsive Peter had nothing to say and was content to let another do the speaking. It is for the imagination, a sacred and blessed field, but each one of us must think of it and picture it for himself.

In a less theological and argumentative form than Paul's, but with warm and tender zeal, Peter in his Letters writes of the Atonement for the sins of man through the death of Christ. "Ye were redeemed," he writes, "not with corruptible things, as silver and gold, from your vain (manner of life) received by tradition from your fathers; but with the precious blood of Christ, as of a lamb without blemish and without spot" (1 Peter 1:18, 19). In the opening note of the doxology, in the first letter, it is difficult not to hear the echo of Peter's own experience —"Blessed be the God and Father of our Lord Jesus Christ, which according to His abundant mercy hath begotten us again unto a lively hope by the resurrection of Jesus Christ from the dead." Was he not thinking how the resurrection of Christ from the dead and His special appearance unto him had been the resurrection of hope in his own heart? The Master he had deserted and denied sought and found him and brought him back into His fold.

"The strongest, whitest, sweetest soul the world has ever known" —thus a celebrated Anglo-American preacher once described Jesus in a New York pulpit. How strange, how very strange, that would sound in a letter of Peter or Paul! They, too, and that in matchless terms, could speak of the lovely traits of the Son of Man. But what constrains their love and indites their song of thanksgiving and gives wings to their hope is not the loveliness of the character of Jesus, but the fact that He died for them and bore their sins in His own Body on the tree. It was belief in that fact that built the Church and that has preserved the Church from the days of Peter down to this present time. The main thing to be said about Peter, and perhaps the most luminous, is that he was a sinner who had been saved by what he himself called "the great mercy" of God.

# JUDAS THE THRICE-NAMED

In Matthew he is called "Lebbæus, whose surname is Thaddæus;" in Mark, Thaddæus; in Acts and in Luke, "Judas of James." Hence he has been called the thrice-named disciple. Our Authorized Version fills in the ellipsis of the Greek text in Luke and Acts, which reads "Judas of James" or "James Judas," by supplying the word "brother." A more likely rendering, however, would be, "Judas the son of James."

All that we know of this disciple is the question he asked Jesus at the Last Supper, one of the four memorable questions that were put to Christ that night. Jesus was trying to comfort His disciples against His death and separation from them. "I will not leave you comfortless: I will come to you. Yet a little while and the world seeth Me no more, but ye see Me: because I live ye shall live also. He that hath My commandments and keepeth them, he it is that loveth Me; and he that loveth Me shall be loved of My Father, and I will love him and will manifest Myself to him" (John 14:18-21).

This puzzled Judas as it must have puzzled all the other disciples. How could Christ appear to His disciples and yet not be seen of others, and even if He could do this, why would He desire to show Himself unto the disciples and not unto the world at large? "Lord, how is it that Thou wilt manifest Thyself unto us, and not unto the world?" (v.22).

After the resurrection, Jesus manifested Himself to His disciples, to many who believed on His Name, but not unto the public at large. Is this what Jesus meant when He said that the world would not see Him but His disciples would see Him? Probably not. Our Lord seems to speak of His spiritual manifestation, not a corporeal one. When He gave them His final commission, He said, "Lo, I am with you alway, even unto the end of the world." There, certainly, He did not mean a corporeal manifestation and presence.

The mistake of Judas had been a very common one among the disciples of Jesus and persists to this day, taking the particular form of emphasis on millennialism and the bodily advent of Christ upon the earth. Not that such an appearance will not take place, but that Christ in the farewell address seeks to comfort the hearts of the disciples by assuring them of His presence with them, manifesting Himself to them in a real and most precious way, so that His disciples should take courage and comfort in Him, although the world saw nothing and believed nothing.

Paul, speaking of his trial at Rome and how his friends forsook him as the disciples had once forsaken their Lord, said, "But the Lord stood with me, and strengthened me; that by me the preaching might be fully known. . . . And the Lord shall deliver me from every evil work, and will preserve me unto His heavenly kingdom" (2 Tim. 4:17,18). Paul knew that Christ was there, manifesting Himself as his helper and friend, though Nero and the soldiers and hangers-on about the court saw nothing and felt nothing.

Great spiritual truth lies wrapped in the somewhat obscure promises about the return of our Lord to this earth in glory and in judgment. But whatever that may be, however we try to get a mental picture of it, there is this other return and presence of Christ, not the Second Advent, but the perennial advent to those who live in Him. We do not need to wait for rending heavens and opening graves and uncovered seas to behold Christ. Even now the eye of faith may perceive Him. "Behold, I stand at the door and knock: if any man hear My voice and open the door, I will come in to him, and will sup with him, and he with Me" (Revelation 3:20).

You may have talked with Christians who have passed through great trial as by fire and who will reverently relate how the Lord Himself stood by them. There was granted unto them a blessed, mighty demonstration of His help and His companionship, an experience which will never fade from their minds. Happy are they who may have had such experience.

But, surely, without claiming such overwhelming demonstration of the presence of Christ, there have been times when you saw the Lord and were helped, you looked unto Him and were not confounded. It may have been as you sat in the church and heard the accents of a hymn of grace that touched your spirit as with an angel's wand; or when your whole being cried a fervent Amen to the declaration of God's saving goodness; or in some sacramental hour of sorrow, or of joy; or at someone's death, when the *Twenty-third Psalm* became a great reality —"Yea, though I walk through the valley of the shadow of death, I will fear no evil, for Thou art with me" —or at someone's birth, when the glory and spirituality of life came like a flood upon your soul, and the eternal Son of God stood, as it were, before you, the Redeemer and the Benefactor of your life.

> Jesus, these eyes have never seen
> That glorious form of Thine;
> The veil of sense hangs dark between
> Thy blessed face and mine.
>
> I see Thee not, I hear Thee not,
> Yet art Thou oft with me;
> And earth hath ne'er so dear a spot
> As where I meet with Thee.
>
> Like some bright dream that comes unsought,
> When slumbers o'er me roll,
> Thine image ever fills my thought,
> And charms my ravished soul.

Yes, the disciples may see Christ when the world sees Him not. The great temptation of Christian disciples today is to be dismayed and affrighted when they learn that the world cannot or will not see Him whom the believer sees. Hence, the half-sad, half-humorous efforts that are made to destroy the supernatural element in the Christian religion, to try and accommodate Christianity to the doubts and skepticism and even to the infidelity of the world.

If your Christian faith is not strong enough to keep you from fear when you find that others deny, even ridicule, all that you have received and believed, your own belief, your own hopes, your own love for Christ and faith in God and hope of forgiveness through His blood and of the life that is to come —they are but poor things indeed, mere reeds shaken with the wind.

The answer of Jesus to the question of Judas, it is to be observed, ignores the thing that troubled Judas, a manifestation to the Twelve but not to the world. Perhaps, at that stage Judas and the others could not receive it (John 16:25). What He does explain in His great answer is the condition upon which a disciple of Christ receives the Divine manifestation and knows in his heart of hearts that Christ is and that He ever liveth to help him and uphold him. That condition is grand in its simplicity—obedience: "If a man love Me, Judas, he will keep My words: and My Father will love him, and we will come unto him, and make our abode with him" (John 14:23).

It is the old law that moral fidelity is the law of spiritual illumination, that if a man does what is right he will come to know what is true. How many times and with what divers tones the Word of God declares this truth which Christ stated to Judas!

"Unto the upright there ariseth light in the darkness" (Psalm 112:4).

"Light is sown for the righteous, and gladness for the upright in heart" (Psalm 97:11),

"The secret of the Lord is with them that fear Him" (Psalm 25:14),

"The path of the just is as the shining light, that shineth more and more unto the perfect day" (Prov. 4:18),

"Blessed are the pure in heart; for they shall see God" (Matt. 5:8).

# THOMAS

The chief thing to remember about Thomas is not that he doubted, that he asked for unusual evidence, but that he was convinced, that he believed so thoroughly and enthusiastically as to give expression to the greatest confession in Christian history, "My Lord and my God!" (John 20:28).

The Psalmist says that God is able to make the wrath of man to praise Him. Here we have an instance of how God can make the doubt of man to praise Him. In the Providence of God, the chief doubter among the apostles becomes the chief defender of the truth of the Resurrection.

The history of Thomas disposes effectually of the foolish and yet much exploited idea that the disciples were a band of silly enthusiasts, ready to believe anything that their affections should dictate. The disciples were not logicians and schooled in the giving of evidence, but they were not a set of fools; they were hard-headed men, disinclined to believe in the Resurrection, much though they desired to see their Master again. When the women told them of the empty sepulchre and the two men in shining garments, "their words seemed to them as idle tales, and they believed them not" (Luke 24:11).

Thomas is the chief representative of this spirit of doubt. In a remarkable manner he was devoted to the Master. When Jesus heard of the sickness of Lazarus and announced to His disciples that He was going to Judæa again (He was then beyond the Jordan), they sought to dissuade Him, reminding Him how the Jews of late tried to stone Him. But Thomas, when he saw that Jesus was determined to go, said, "Let us also go, that we may die with Him' (John 11:16).

Who, then, more than this disciple, who was ready to die with Jesus and exhorted His companions to a like loyalty —who more than he could have desired to see Jesus rise again from the dead? But, in spite of that devotion and in spite of that desire, the Resurrection was such a tremendous event that Thomas was sorrowfully skeptical about it. He even, somewhat haughtily, rejected the testimony of his fellow-disciples and declared that he must not only see Christ in the flesh, but that he must examine His wounds so as to establish beyond all peradventure of a doubt that this was his Master who had been crucified. This is the man who, when Jesus meets him, cries out, "My Lord and my God!"

Without any warrant for it whatsoever, Thomas has been called the Rationalist of the Apostolic Band. He is likened to men who claim a superior endowment of intelligence because they set themselves to doubt what others believe. In any company of twelve men where eleven of them believe, the one who doubts will, by his very singularity, attract great attention to himself. The doubters among men have attracted undue attention to themselves, not because of their superior ability, but because of their singularity, and too often the desire to dissent is mistaken for convictions grounded upon careful study and superior judgment.

The rationalist, the ordinary sceptic, as we think of him and as we experience him, is not looking for signs of truth in Christianity but for signs of its falsehood. He will ferret out some little seeming discrepancy of the biblical records and magnify it into a mountain, whereas the mighty panorama of Christian history and influence fades into nothingness.

A friend once said to Grant when he was President that Sumner did not believe in the Bible. "Of course," answered General Grant, "Sumner doesn't believe in the Bible: He didn't write it." That attitude of mind towards Christian truth, however justly or unjustly imputed to the brilliant senator from New England, is typical of many of those who vent their doubts loudly and boast that they do not accept anything the way other people do but must have infallible proofs. There are some people who would never believe in any Bible that they themselves did not write.

Thomas, it is true, asked for signs, for particular evidence, but to liken him to the rationalist, to the sceptic, in the common use of that term is to do him a great injustice and to wrest the Scriptures. The difference between the rationalist and Thomas is this: the rationalist wants to disbelieve; Thomas wanted to believe. The rationalist, of the honest type, is occasioned by study, by examination of evidence, by the pressing bounds of the natural world, making the other world seem unreal; but the doubt of Thomas was the doubt born of sorrow.

This is the deepest doubt of all, the doubt born of sorrow; that is, the doubt which rises out of the experience of our lives. The great doubts are not those that are born, in the study of the critic, in the debate of religions, nor are they born in the laboratory, from the study of the laws of nature; they are not born of meditating over the rocks and the stars and the planets, of tracing out genealogies and chronologies; they are born in the library and in the laboratory of the soul; they are the dark interrogations cast by the experiences through which we pass in this strange adventure men call life.

The doubt of a man who talks of the impossibility of a Virgin Birth is one thing; but let it not be confused with the doubt of a mother who has lost her firstborn child and wonders if God is, and if her child still lives. The doubt of a man who questions the Mosaic account of the Creation of the world is one thing, but let it not be confused with the doubt of the man who sees the world in travail and sore anguish, the ceaseless invasion of hate and the eternal enmity of the evil for the good, the inhumanity of man to man, and wonders if God has forsaken His world.

The doubt of Thomas was not that of a quibbler, of a cold-blooded, dilettante student; it was the doubt of a man who had lost his Lord and Master. Sorrow had filled his heart. Had his doubt been of that former nature, mere asking for signs or proofs, Jesus would have answered him as He did those other doubters, calling them a wicked and adulterous generation, seeking after a sign. Thomas was not a Sadducee; there is no evidence that he disbelieved in the resurrection as it was commonly held in Israel at that time; that is, he was no professional doubter in a resurrection. But when he was confronted with the death of Jesus, the doubt of sorrow overwhelmed him.

On no other ground can we understand the exquisite, tender manner in which Jesus dealt with him, giving him all that he asked. Nor do I think that Thomas searched the wounds of his Master, as he had declared he must do before he could or would believe. The majestic presence of the Risen Christ like a flood swept away all his doubts and, falling at His feet, he cried in adoration, in belief, and in penitence, "My Lord and my God!"

The greatness of Leonardo's conception of the Twelve grew upon me as I studied it from day to day. And among all these masterly representations, I think that of Thomas is *facile princeps*. Look into his face and at once you have the true Thomas; not the Sadducee, the rationalist, the carping critic, but the man of intense affection, with that earnest, yearning nature touched with the past cast of melancholy. Things troubled Thomas that did not trouble other disciples. But Jesus stooped to his infirmity. As if He anticipated the overpraise of Thomas as a sceptic and the neglect of him as a believer, and an undue valuation for the proof of signs and demonstration, Jesus said to Thomas, "Thomas, because thou hast seen Me, thou hast believed: blessed are they that have not seen, and yet have believed" (John 20:29). Jesus did not mean to discount intelligent faith, nor did He put a premium upon easy, unquestioning faith. Nor did He mean to teach that future believers who could not have the evidence afforded Thomas would be happier, more blessed in their faith than was Thomas. It would be difficult to conceive of any Christian more happy, more blessed, more convinced than was Thomas when he fell at the feet of Christ with his memorable confession.

In that prophecy of the bliss of future believers, Jesus both set the superior worth of evidence that is not founded on visible manifestations —seeing the Lord in the flesh, beholding His wounds —the evidence of faith and the witness of the Spirit, and foretold the joy and happiness which would be the lot of those who hereafter should believe on His Name. The experience of Thomas is "useful," as Dr. Robert Ellis Thompson writes, "but not ideal." It is not ideal, for we cannot have that kind of evidence for which Thomas asked, neither is that kind of evidence the highest. Christian faith is more than an infallible demonstration: it is the loving venture of the heart, our trust in Christ.

# BARTHOLOMEW

Of all the apostles of whose call to follow Jesus there is left us a record in the Gospels, Bartholomew was the only one who hesitated. All the others rose up at once and followed. Bartholomew was not convinced when the first invitation came to him through Philip, and even when he met Jesus he had some question to ask Him before he became His disciple (John 1:46-49).

But, just as Thomas doubted concerning the resurrection of Christ only to come at length to a belief in it which expressed itself in the greatest confession in Christian history, so Bartholomew hesitated at first about becoming the disciple of Jesus but ended by hailing Him as the Son of God.

From the foregoing it will be seen that I identify Nathanael with Bartholomew. It cannot be proven that they are one and the same person. The reason for so thinking is the fact that Matthew, Mark, and Luke in their enumeration of the Twelve speak of Bartholomew but not of a Nathanael, whereas John tells of Nathanael but knows nothing of Bartholomew. John relates how Philip brought Nathanael to Jesus, and in the lists of the Twelve in the other three Gospels Philip and Nathanael are always mentioned together. It is thus altogether probable that the Nathanael of John is the Bartholomew of Matthew, Mark, and Luke —Nathanael being his chief name and Bartholomew indicating his filial relationship, meaning son of Tolmai.

The finest natures sometimes surprise us with their bondage of prejudice. On all other subjects fair and generous, there will be one subject upon which they are unreasonable and the children of prejudice. Bartholomew was not a slave to prejudice, but he was subject to its influence, for when Philip sought him out and said to him, "We have found Him of whom Moses in the law, and the prophets did write, Jesus of Nazareth, the son of Joseph;" Bartholo-

mew answered, "Can there any good thing come out of Nazareth?" The reply has become proverbial, expressing one's disbelief in noble or distinguished qualities in certain persons or worthy characters from certain places.

As Bartholomew was himself a Galilean, perhaps it was not so much from pride and scorn, as might have been the case with a Judæan, that he raised this question about Nazareth, as from an unworthy humility. He had come to share in the sentiments entertained beyond the borders of his province that nothing good nor great could ever come out of Galilee, especially that little town of Nazareth, and least of all the Messiah of Israel. But the fine thing about Bartholomew is that he did not allow this scepticism, or prejudice, whichever you like to call it, to interfere with him listening to the proof that Philip had to offer for his affirmation that he had found the Messiah.

And what was that proof? Only this: "Come and see." Christianity has nothing to hide. It has no doctrines that must be kept in the background. It would win no disciples under false pretense of being something that it is not. Jesus reveals Himself to men. He says, with Philip, "Come and see."

The prejudice which exists in the mind of humanity towards the Gospel and the Saviour of the Gospel, an indubitable prejudice, is an indirect tribute to its truth and its merit. The Gospel declares itself to be a message of good tidings, all that is good for man, but it also declares that the heart of man is enmity against God, that man has prejudices against his best friend. And not all who are prejudiced against the Gospel have the candor of this hesitating disciple who came and saw and believed.

In answer to the laconic reply of Philip, Bartholomew went with him to see Jesus. Jesus, seeing him coming, exclaimed, "Behold an Israelite indeed, in whom there is no guile!" This is another saying from this celebrated account of the call of Bartholomew that has passed into the proverbial speech of our day, making the name of Bartholomew a synonym for sincerity. Jesus had in this disciple a solid foundation upon which to build.

This guileless, open-hearted, open-minded Bartholomew was astonished that Jesus would presume to pass judgment upon his character when He had never known, possibly had never seen him, before. "Whence knowest Thou me?" Jesus answered, "Before that Philip called thee, when thou wast under the fig tree, I saw thee." Then Bartholomew said, "Rabbi, Thou art the Son of God, Thou art the King of Israel!"

At first reading, this looks as if Bartholomew was amazed that Jesus had the power to read a man's mind and that by preternatural knowledge He knew that he had been sitting under a fig tree. If this is all, then Bartholomew believes that Jesus is the Son of God simply because He possesses a strange power of telepathy and vision.

But I think that there is far more here than that. It was not that Jesus knew his physical location, sitting under a fig tree, but that He knew his spiritual location, knew all that was in his heart as he sat musing and praying beneath the fig tree, understood all the pure aspirations of his heart. It was this which made Bartholomew feel that he had to deal with no ordinary person, yea, that the Son of God stood in the flesh before him. It was a case of "deep calling unto deep."

That is the strange, spiritual power of Jesus Christ, that He needs not that man should testify of man, or that man should testify of himself, for He knows what is in man. Bartholomew perceived how Jesus knew all the hopes and longings of his heart, the holy aspirations of his meditations, without his telling Him, and he cried out, "Thou art the Son of God!" The woman of Samaria heard Jesus tell her how many husbands she had had and the state in which she was then living, and, awed and impressed, said, "Sir, I perceive that Thou art a prophet." The great truth envisaged in the conversion of Bartholomew is that Christ is the soul's true Mate, true Companion.

Test this by your own hearts beneath the fig tree. There have been hours when the blessed mood hinted at by Wordsworth has come upon you; when mist and cloud seemed to have been swept aside, and you realized to the full your spiritual nature, your spiritual inheritance.

> That blessed mood,
> In which the burthen of the mystery,
> In which the heavy and the weary weight
> Of all this unintelligible world
> Is lightened: that serene and blessed mood,
> In which the affections gently lead us on,
> Until, the breath of this corporeal frame
> And even the motion of our human blood
> Almost suspended, we are laid asleep
> In body, and become a living soul:
> While with an eye made quiet by the power
> Of harmony and the deep power of joy,
> We see into the life of things.

The fears of life no longer haunted you; the cares of life no more harassed you; the vain strivings of life were stilled. The soul looked duty and destiny straight in the eye and flinched not. A hunger and thirst after righteousness, a desire to be without sin or guile, a mighty yearning for whatsoever things that are high and holy and pure and lovely and of good report came upon you like a swelling flood.

Then you thought of Christ, or afterwards you heard of Christ, and at once you recognized in Him the fullness of all that for which you had dreamed or sighed. He was your One altogether lovely, the chiefest among ten thousand. In Him the vague, wandering aspirations took form and shape, as with the African savage, who listening to the missionary's story of the Cross and Him who died thereon, exclaimed, "I always knew that there must be such a Saviour!"

We are troubled by the doubts that rise from our own minds. But let us not forget that the Lord knoweth them that are His and, what is more, that the sheep hear His voice, that thousands of Christian disciples are finding Christ the One of whose existence their best hopes and aspirations had ever told them; that the deeps in man are ever calling unto the deeps of God, that in Christ men discover their true spiritual homeland.

'Tis the weakness in strength that I cry for! My flesh, that I seek
In the Godhead! I seek and I find it. O Saul, it shall be
A Face like my face that receives thee; a Man like to me,
Thou shalt love and be loved by, forever: a Hand like this hand
Shall throw open the gates of new life to thee! See the Christ stand!

# JAMES

Seventeen years before the day of his execution, James and his brother John had asked for seats of honor in the kingdom of Christ. Jesus asked them if they were ready to pay the price. Could they be baptized with His baptism? Could they drink His cup? Eagerly and impulsively, if ignorantly, they had answered, "We are able."

Now for James the final test had come. Over him flashed the persecuting sword of Herod Agrippa, the brother of that Herodias who had been the cause of the death of John the Baptist. The bitter chalice was pressed to the lips of James and he drank it in the faith and spirit of His Master. James was not

> The martyr first, whose eagle eye
> Could pierce beyond the grave,
> Who saw his Master in the sky,
> And called on Him to save,

for the distinction of wearing the first martyr's crown belongs to the pious and eloquent Stephen. But the first of the apostles to die was James. Hence he is called the proto-martyr.

The lips of the evangelist are sealed as to the manner of the death of James. We would like to think, indeed we can think, that this James, who once asked permission to call down fire on bigoted and inhospitable Samaritans, knew better now the spirit that he was of, and that, softened and purified by the

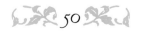

memories of Jesus, he went to his death like Stephen with a prayer for "them that did the wrong."

It is very singular that James' own brother John never once mentions him in his long Gospel, nor aside from the story of his martyrdom do we hear of him in the book of the Acts, save in a catalogue of the apostles. We might dismiss him as one of the least important of the Twelve; but the fact of his being picked out for the sword by Herod shows that James occupied a most notable position as an apostle. Herod killed him in order to please the Jews, and in selecting his victim he would choose an outstanding figure in the band of Christian disciples. Moreover, the next apostle whom he marked for the slaughter was none other than Peter. The silence, then, of John and the comparative silence of the Acts is not to be taken to mean that James was not a leading figure in the band of apostles.

He was the first of the Twelve to taste of death. Judas tasted of death even before Christ was crucified; but now we leave him out of the reckoning and, counting Matthias in the place of Judas, James is, apart from all personal traits, brought prominently before us because of the Twelve he was the first to die. The first to die! This was a band of friends, a family, as it were. Now death invades that home and the one for whom he calls first is James.

Sometimes it is John, sometimes Peter, sometimes Henry, sometimes Robert, sometimes Mary, sometimes Sarah —but always there is a first. Strong, rugged brothers grow and thrive and toil for long years and never think of death as a thing related to them. Then one day comes the tidings, "James is very sick; James died last night." So runs the history of all families, of all earthly groups and associations, of all graduating classes —always a first to feel the edge of death's sharp sword. Oh thank God for families! If you have had brothers and sisters and are blessed with many of them, thank Heaven for it and show your gratitude by kindness to your own.

All that John and Peter and Matthew and the rest could do when they heard that James was dead was to take up his body and give it decent sepulture. Did they think now of any kindness they might have shown James? Did John recall how he might have been a little more thoughtful concerning that elder brother of his? Was there anything that ought to have been done before Herod's sword flashed and fell? We know not. But if there were, it could now never, never be done. In this matter, in this great matter of family relationship, the duties and privileges of brothers and friends, whatsoever thy hand findeth to do, do it now and with thy might. With thy might! Life's transitoriness and brevity demand all thy might in this matter, for when falls the sword of the inevitable and inexorable Herod of Death, then all thy might and all thy tears and all thy repentance will avail thee nothing.

Comparing Matthew 27:56 with Mark 15:40, we are justified in thinking that the "mother of the sons of Zebedee" and Salome are one and the same person. In St. John's list of the women at the Cross (John 19:25), "His mother's sister" is mentioned. It has been conjectured that this was Salome, and thus James and John would be cousins of Jesus.

We know that James' mother was a strong-minded woman, ambitious for her sons, for although Mark says that James and John made the request that they might sit, one on the right hand and the other on the left of Jesus in His Kingdom, St. Matthew says that the request was made through their mother. Remarkable men have back of them remarkable mothers, and Salome must have been such a woman. She was at fault in the manner of her request, nevertheless it was a place in the Kingdom of Christ that she asked for her children; it was near Him that she yearned to see her sons.

But what of James' father? Zebedee was his name, a prosperous fish merchant of Capernaum. His class was good. As one has said, he "came from that vigorous lower middle class which has furnished so many effective workers for the cause of God and humanity in all ages—a class not so far removed from the danger of want as to be able to relax its energies and sink down into self-indulgence, but yet not so bound down to drudgery as to lose heart and inspiration for subjects beyond the daily routine of toil." Salome became one of the women who attended Jesus upon His journeys, supported Him with their substance, stood afar off beholding His Cross and wept at His sepulchre; but of Zebedee we hear nothing further.

We like to think that he, too, became a disciple of Jesus and that this James is a representative of one of those Christian homes in which all the members are followers of the Lamb. It is a blessed thing when it is so. Who, having once tasted, can speak lightly of the joy of being in a home where father and mother, brothers and sisters are all friends of Christ?

Robert Burns strikes this note when he makes the old father in *The Cottar's Saturday Night* thus pray to heaven for the redemption of all his children and their reunion in heaven:

Then kneeling down to Heaven's Eternal King,
   The saint, the father and the husband prays:
Hope "springs exulting on triumphant wing,"
   That thus they all shall meet in future days,
There, ever bask in uncreated rays,
   No more to sigh, or shed the bitter tear,
Together hymning their Creator's praise,
   In such society, yet still more dear;
While circling time moves round in an eternal sphere.

James was one of three disciples admitted to a special intimacy with Christ. He saw Him transfigured, he saw Him raise the dead, he was taken apart with Him in Gethsemane. Yet James, as well as Peter and John, frequently manifests a spirit that had little to do with that of Christ.

The most striking instance of this was when a Samaritan village refused to show Jesus hospitality or grant a place to rest because He and His companions were Jews. This insult brought to the surface all the flaming wrath of the Sons of Thunder, and they requested permission to call down fire from heaven upon the inhospitable village.

The descendants of James and John have been legion. They have done what Jesus did not permit these fiery apostles to do; they have called down flames of devastation and destruction upon those races and creeds and nations and cities which refused to receive them or adopt their opinions.

There is an old legend of Abraham which teaches its lesson of toleration. Sitting one day at the door of his tent, he was visited by a stranger. Abraham asked him within and they sat down to break bread together. Unlike Abraham, the stranger did not pause to ask a blessing. Abraham inquired the reason why, and he told him that he worshipped the sun. Angry with him, Abraham drove him out of the tent. Afterwards the Lord called and asked where the stranger was. Abraham replied, "I thrust him out because he did not worship Thee." Then said the Lord: "I have suffered him and his ancestors for hundreds of years, and couldst not thou endure him for one hour?" When we grow angry with those who differ with us, wishing them eliminated from the families of the earth, let us remember that God has suffered them, yea, that He has suffered generation after generation of sinners upon the face of the earth. We can afford to be as tolerant as God.

For the love of God is broader
    Than the measures of man's mind,
And the heart of the Eternal
    Is most wonderfully kind:
But we make His love too narrow
    By false limits of our own,
And we magnify His strictness
    With a zeal He will not own.

The danger today is not always that of intolerance; it is quite frequently the danger of indifference. If men are in earnest about their faith they will contend for it. Christ did not choose weaklings for the inner band of His friends, but strong, mercurial, impulsive men. James and John He surnamed Boanerges, Sons of Thunder. Sometimes their ardor carried them too far, as in this instance of the Samaritan village; but within bounds it was a noble and worthy trait, this ability to be volcanic, to thunder, to talk like Elijah.

"He was incapable of moral indignation" was the comment made upon one of our American ambassadors who died some time ago. He was a gifted man, but Jesus would never have chosen him for the apostolate. The highest manhood must be capable of indignation, it must know how to kindle and flare with righteous anger. Better the misdirected zeal of James and John than the smiles and caresses of the indifferent.

Anger is a great virtue; even God is represented as at times an angry God. That means that man and God can feel deeply. But anger uncontrolled, or not evoked by just occasion, is a menace to the soul and can do injury wherever its flame consumes. Be angry, but sin not.

But do not fear to be a Son of Thunder. Christ desired such men for His disciples. I have no doubt that the reason why the Jews desired the death of James before all the other apostles, and therefore why Herod chose him for the sword, was because James had spoken great, plain, burning words there in Jerusalem, such as only a Son of Thunder knew how to speak.

As Carlyle wrote of John Knox, "Tolerance has to tolerate the unessential and see well what that is. Tolerance has to be noble, just, measured in its wrath, when it can tolerate no longer. But on the whole, we are not here altogether to tolerate. We are here to resist, to control, to vanquish withal.

We do not tolerate Falsehoods, Thieveries, Iniquities, when they fasten upon us; we say to them, Thou art false, thou art not tolerable!''

# JOHN

If there is any failure in the sketches which make up the painting of the Last Supper, I feel that failure is St. John. Leonardo da Vinci succeeds least of all with that disciple who is the greatest and most gifted personality in the entire group. There is hardly a fault that we can find with his conception of Peter, Judas, Philip, James or the rest. But he has represented John as a full-faced, effeminate youth, with something of a Mona Lisa smile on his lips, his white hands meekly and languidly clasped together, and his head inclined towards Judas, around whose shoulder Peter, with the knife in his right hand, is beckoning to John to ask Jesus whom He meant when He said that one of them should that night betray Him.

There is, perhaps, the suggestion of a dreamy introspection, but very little to suggest the John of the Apocalypse, whose emblem is the eagle flying, like John's great angel, in the sun and "kindling his undazzled eye at the full midday beam"; and nothing at all to suggest that blazing Son of Thunder who wished to call down fire on the inhospitable Samaritan village, immortal for its incivility, and who, although he could employ the terms of love and affection, knew how to call the enemies of truth and of Christ "liars" and warn the Church against them.

Jesus loved John. Four times in the Gospel of John we have him described as the disciple whom Jesus loved. Did He not love the others? We know that He did, for John himself in his report of the last night with Christ tells how, "having loved His own which were in the world, He loved them unto the end" (John 13:1).

What, then, are we to make of this oft-repeated statement about the regard that Jesus had for John? The only explanation is that on the side of His human nature Jesus gave full play to His natural affections, but in a way that never excites the anger or the jealousy of the disciples. Peter, James, and John enjoyed a peculiar intimacy, and John had a place all to himself. There was something in the youth that attracted Jesus and made easy the exchange of spirit.

We think of John as the one who, above all the rest, had deep spiritual insight and a quick and easy apprehension of the mystery of God in Christ. These traits appear in his Gospel and his Epistles, and it may have been because he was the first to catch the meaning of Christ, to understand how He was the Eternal Son of God and how He came to give life, that Jesus showed unusual affection for him. We like those who get our meaning quickly, whose thoughts range in the same atmosphere, and who do not, like Philip, need to have every step and every figure explained.

But another explanation of the marked affection which Jesus bore to John may lie in the altogether probable fact that John was the Benjamin of this family of disciples. As such Leonardo represents him, a youth among middle-aged men. Since the record generally reads, not John and James, but James and John, the inference is that John was a younger brother. It is possible too that there was a wide gap between James and John, for even in households today it would not be difficult to find brothers who are separated by almost a score of years. He was certainly younger than Peter and easily outran him on the way to the sepulchre. It may have been because of his youth that he was permitted to pass unchallenged into the court of Annas the high priest. St. John's explanation is that he was "known unto the high priest"; but this need not dismiss the fact that his youth made them pay little attention to him, while Peter had to stay without until John spoke in his behalf and brought him in. Beyond all this is the very trustworthy tradition that John lived to extreme old age, finally ending his witness on earth in the time of Trajan.

The youngest member of any large family is the object of a great deal of advice and commands on the part of his seniors, but also of affection. The mere fact that he is the youngest makes them look upon him a little differently from the way they do upon one another. In times of illness and sorrow there is a medicine in the unconscious ministry of little children; and in grave and serious days of waiting or watching, of famine or siege, full-grown men relieve their spirits by friendly companionship with youth. The innocence, the guilelessness, the enthusiasm of youth constitutes a balm for the anxiety and strain of maturity.

I like to think of John as playing such a part in the band of apostles. For that reason Jesus loved him, and probably all the others loved him, too.

The John whom we see in the Gospels is a youth; but the John who wrote the Apocalypse and the Gospel and the Letters is a full-grown man, perhaps an aged man. It is altogether probable that when John died, the last of all those who had companied with Jesus from the beginning, from the time of the preaching of John the Baptist, had passed from the earth.

Browning's *Death in the Desert* is the poet's imagination of what John might have said, or ought to have said, when he was dying. On the whole, the poem does gross injustice to him who spake so cleverly and wrote so simply, and for lucidity of thought and simplicity of style, Browning had studied John to no purpose. But here and there he makes John say something sensible and comprehensible. One instance is where John refers to his great age and how when he dies the last eye-witness will be gone.

> If I live yet, it is for good, more love
> Through men to men: be naught but ashes here
> That keeps awhile my semblance, who was John—
> Still, when they scatter, there is left on earth
> No one alive who knew (consider this!),
> Saw with his eyes and handled with his hands
> That which was from the first the Word of Life.
> How will it be when none more saith, "I saw"?

It is evidently from the vantage point of great age that John writes when he composes the First Epistle, for he commences by saying, "That which was from the beginning, which we have heard, which we have seen with our eyes, which we have looked upon, and our hands have handled, of the Word of Life . . . that which we have seen and heard declare we unto you, that ye also may have fellowship with us" (1 John 1:1,3). But at length the day had to come for the Church when the last prop of this sort fell away and it had to stand by its own inner strength and by the word of tradition.

"How will it be when none more saith, 'I saw'?"

Jesus Himself has answered that question, for John writes in his Gospel how Jesus said to Thomas, "Because thou hast seen Me, thou hast believed:

blessed are they that have not seen, and yet have believed" (John 20:29).

It is a remarkable thing that John, who is so retiring and modest about speaking of himself, never once calling himself by name in the Gospel, but always either speaking of himself in the third person or hiding his identity by a phrase such as "the disciple whom Jesus loved"—should never once refer to any of those incidents in the story of his discipleship which give an unfavorable impression of his character.

That there were such incidents we know from the other Gospels. Upon three different occasions John spoke or acted so as to bring upon him the rebuke of Jesus. Mark tells us that after Jesus had given the disciples an illustrated sermon on humility by taking a child in His arms, John came to him and said that they had seen a man casting out evil spirits in the Name of Jesus and that they had forbidden him. Very likely John or James did the forbidding. John expects Jesus to commend him, but Jesus rebuked him, saying, "There is no man which shall do a miracle in My Name, that can lightly speak evil of Me. For he that is not against us is on our part" (Mark 9:39.40).

The incident reminds one of a similar occasion in the time of Moses. "And the Lord came down in a cloud, and spake unto him, and took of the spirit that was upon him and gave it unto the seventy elders; and it came to pass, that, when the spirit rested upon them, they prophesied, and did not cease. But there remained two of the men in the camp, the name of the one was Eldad, and the name of the other Medad; and the spirit rested upon them; and they were of them that were written, but went not out unto the tabernacle: and they prophesied in the camp. And there ran a young man, and told Moses, and said, Eldad and Medad do prophesy in the camp. And Joshua the son of Nun, the servant of Moses, one of his young men, answered and said, My Lord Moses, forbid them. And Moses said unto him, Enviest thou for my sake? Would God that all the Lord's people were prophets, and that the Lord would put his spirit upon them!" (Number 11:25-29).

John had the spirit of exclusiveness which has misrepresented Christ to the world. He was of the spirit of Joshua who would have no prophesying outside of the sacred precinct, which was not according to the common usage, and called upon Moses to suppress it. The noble answer of Moses was like unto the answer of Jesus to John and of the answer of Paul fifteen hundred years after Moses, when the Jews were so frightened because Christ was being preached outside their church and custom, "What then? notwithstanding, every way, whether in pretense, or in truth, Christ is preached; and I therein do rejoice, yea, and will rejoice" (Philippians 1:18).

Another instance of the narrow spirit of John was his joining with James in asking power to call down fire on the Samaritan village which had showed incivility to their Master. It was the abuse of that which was good. Jesus liked the mercurial, blazing disposition of these two brothers, but His labor was to train them and refine them so that they could use this splendid quality of righteous indignation to better purposes.

John never altogether lost those qualities which made Jesus call him a Son of Thunder. Such a man was best fitted to be the medium through which should come the fearful revelation of the symbols of Divine wrath and judgment. It was to the Son of Thunder, not to Leonardo's simpering weakling, that the Lord showed the "things that must shortly come to pass."

Tradition tells us, though uncertainly, that John, too, suffered martyrdom, thus drinking the cup that he said, so eagerly, he was able to drink, but understanding now far better the meaning of the cup and the way to honor and distinction in the Kingdom of Heaven.

There are beautiful legends, too, about John tracing a former young disciple, who had fallen away and become chief of a robber band, to his fastness and winning him back to Christ; and of his hurrying from the bath in which he had discovered Cerinthus the heretic, lest the roof should fall upon him; of his tame partridge and of his oft-repeated blessing, when borne by the strong arms of his young men into the Christian assemblage, he lifted his withered arms and said, "Little children, love one another."

John Milton has a great passage in which he gives us his idea of what the character of a poet ought to be. He says: "He who would not be frustrated of his hope to write well ought himself to be a true poem —not presuming to sing high praises of heroic men and women or famous cities, unless he have in himself the experience and practice of all that which is praiseworthy."

In the Apocalypse John gives us the vision of the future. Many of the symbols and emblems perplex and puzzle us; but always the book is radiant with the light of moral splendor. Back of the great book was the great life of the Apostle. As in the book the thunders of judgment alternate with the overtures of mercy and the accents of peace, so in the life of John there was rainbow round about the throne. A veritable Son of Thunder, yet tender and affectionate, leaning upon the breast of Jesus and taking into his arms the weeping Mary with the sword through her heart, and faithless Peter too.

If to John much was given, let it be remembered that John loved much. If to John was granted the vision of the things of the future, unfolding the majesty and the glory, the judgments and the mercy of God, let it be remembered that John was himself in the Spirit when the vision came to him. His holy life was the preparation for the glorious vision. It is John who preserves for us the word of Jesus that if any man love Him He will come unto him. He is the illustration of that promise. "Beloved, let us love one another: for love is of God; and everyone that loveth is born of God, and knoweth God. He that loveth not knoweth not God; for God is love" (1 John 4:7,8).

We have not read many verses of the prologue to John's Gospel before we realize that we are dealing with a very great document, not only, as with the other Gospels, because of the great facts set forth, but because of the discussion of the meaning of the facts. When John writes, the first blush of the Christian enthusiasm has commenced to fade and the age of interpretation and theology has commenced.

I venture to say that if the average Christian takes up the Gospels one by one and tries to read them through at a sitting, he will find that the Gospel of John will weary him sooner than any of them. This is due to the fact that the Gospel is made up, for the most part, of a series of discourses of Jesus growing out of incidents in His ministry. With all the comfort and help that you get out of these discourses there is much in them that is dark, mysterious, and inexplicable. The sentiment in your mind is very often precisely that to which His hearers, whether His own disciples or angry Scribes and Pharisees, gave expression, "What does He mean?"

We hear Him tell Nicodemus about the new birth and we say, "How can these things be?" We hear Him tell the Jews that "except ye eat the flesh of the Son of man and drink His blood, ye have no life in yourselves," and with the Jews we say, "How can this man give us His flesh to eat?" Or with the disciples, "This is a hard saying, who can hear it?" Even in that touching farewell address, how much there is amid those blessed sentences of comfort and hope which are still enigmas to you and me. We sympathize with Thomas when he interrupted Christ and said, "We know not whither Thou goest, and how can we know the way?" "In that day," said Christ, "ye shall ask Me nothing" (John 16:23). That day has not yet come, and still many of these sayings of Christ are what He Himself termed them, "dark sayings" (John 16:25, RV).

Least of all to our taste are those prolonged discussions which Jesus had with the Jewish leaders at Jerusalem about His rank, His relationship to the Father, and His relationship to the world. There Christ appears more as a theological antagonist than as the Great Teacher and Physician of the other Gospels.

But as different as the style of these addresses in the Fourth Gospel are, we have no difficulty at all in discerning in them the same Christ whom we see in the other Gospels. Much of the difference in tone and manner is to be accounted for by the difference in aim that John had, not primarily to write a narrative of the life of Jesus, for that had been well done, but to gather together proofs of His divinity and Messiahship. John's Gospel is a clear-cut statement of the fundamental truth of Christianity that the Son of God became man, taking to Himself a true body and a reasonable soul.

As long as Christians hold to that they have a peculiar and glorious religion. As soon as they forget it, they begin to fall into the morass of pantheism, and the various other 'isms and cults that have sprung up like Cadmus' teeth. That Jesus is the Eternal Son of God, that He became flesh and dwelt among us, that He died on the Cross for our sins, that He rose from the dead, that by believing in Him we have life eternal —there the whole Christian structure stands or falls. Wherever that is gone, we have only the name of Christianity, but not its substance.

What makes John's Gospel beloved to the Church, however, is not its great apology for the divinity of Jesus Christ, but its ministry of comfort and hope to the disciple's heart. Our Lord's words as He sat by the well of Jacob to the woman of Samaria, "Whosoever drinketh of the water that I shall give him shall never thirst," fall sweetly on the believer's ears, as sweetly as those other words of the Gospel of Matthew, "Come unto Me all ye that labor and are heavy laden, and I will give you rest. Take My yoke upon you; and learn of Me; for I am meek and lowly in heart: and ye shall find rest unto your souls. For My yoke is easy, and My burden is light." If Luke and Matthew give us the parable of the Lost Sheep, it is John who tells us of the Good Shepherd and the sheepfold, and how Christ is the Good Shepherd because He lay down His life for the sheep. The others tell us of Jairus' daughter and the widow of Nain's son, but it is John, in his story of Lazarus and Mary and

Martha, who tells the perfect story of the tender pathos of the house of mourning, the heartache of sorrow, touched by the hope of life eternal.

But most precious of all is what the writer of the hymn has called "His tender last farewell." This farewell address and last prayer of Jesus are preserved for us by John in the last part of his Gospel. If we wonder why John forsook Galilee's shores for the precincts of the temple and preferred to record the disputes between Jesus and the Pharisees concerning His nature and claims to those other sayings of Jesus about purity and meekness and patience and kindness —we can never be thankful enough that he preserved for us the last words of Jesus to His disciples and the great prayer which He offered for Himself, for the whole Church in every age and among every people.

There we hear the new commandment that we love one another, "even as I have loved you." There our relationship to Him is described under the beautiful figure of the vine and its branches, "I am the vine, ye are the branches." There the promise of the Holy Spirit's presence and guidance in the Church is given. There is given the solemn prophecy of suffering and tribulation in this world, but also the assurance of victory through Him who has overcome the world. There we hear Him pray for the unity of the Church, "that they all may be one, as Thou, Father, art in Me, and I in Thee." There we have a vision of the final glory of all who believe, for there Christ prays that we may all be where He is and behold His glory. There, too, we hear the reading of the last will and testament of our Saviour, and realize how not as the world giveth, He gives unto us. The world gives unrest, disquiet, but Christ gives peace. "Peace I leave with you; My peace I give unto you."

And there, when sorrow's driving rain beats against the window of the soul, and death's fearful victory and piercing sting seem to have written across all our hopes and occupations and yearnings and achievements and affections, one dark word, "Vanity," and fears are in the way, and all the daughters of life's music are brought low —we hear those words at which arms grow strong and hearts grow brave, those most loved by His Church of all the words of life that fell from Immanuel's lips —"Let not your heart be troubled; ye believe in God, believe also in Me. In My Father's house are many mansions; if it were not so, I would have told you. I go to prepare a place for you. And if I go and prepare a place for you, I will come again and will receive you unto Myself; that where I am, there ye may be also."

# MATTHEW

I call Matthew, by way of description, the "publican," for that was his own account of himself. Mark and Luke, in their catalogues of the disciples, call him just Matthew with no descriptive or qualifying words. But Matthew in his own enumeration of the Twelve (Matthew 10:3), when he comes to name himself, writes, "Matthew the publican." It has little meaning for remote ears today, but it meant a great deal for any man to be called a publican in Matthew's day, and it meant a great deal of humility, of unfeigned sorrow, yet of abounding joy, too, over his change of state and fortune, for Matthew to put himself down as a "publican."

A publican! No name was so hateful to the Jews of that day, for no office was so detested. "Publicans and sinners" was the common saying of the people then. It was equivalent; a symbol of degradation, of loss of character and self-respect, of public scorn and contempt. It was the publican's business to collect the taxes imposed by the Roman government. He was thus a representative of the rulers and enslavers of Israel.

His title was a title of infamy, for he was the underling of the wealthy Roman officers who farmed the taxes, paying so much for the privilege of collecting the taxes in a given district, and then gouging out of the people, their helpless victims, as much as they could in excess of the contract price. The burden of taxation was heavy upon the people, who had to satisfy the cupidity of their native rulers and also that of the Roman empire. The income of Herod the Great is said to have been 1,600 talents, or $3,400,000. Any man who held this post of tax collector was bound to be hated by the people, but double was the hatred and scorn when the office was held by a member of their own race, and still worse, when that Hebrew, as in the case of Matthew, was a member of the sacred tribe of Levi.

Jesus had come to "His own city"; that is, Capernaum, His adopted home. He was in the house of Peter, or some other house, when it was noised abroad that He was there and a great crowd gathered within and without. As Jesus was preaching to them, four men brought one that was sick of the palsy, and, unable to get near Jesus for the press of the crowd, they uncovered the roof and let down the sick man before Him. And Jesus healed him.

Leaving the crowded house and congested highway Jesus went forth again by the seaside, and as he passed by He saw Matthew sitting at the receipt of custom and "He said unto him, 'Follow Me.' And he left all, rose up, and followed Him" (Luke 5:27, 28).

I like to think that Matthew, like the other publican who came to Christ, Zacchaeus, was a rich man, and when Luke writes that "he left all" it means that Matthew forsook a lucrative, if ignoble, calling for the humble friendship of Christ. He probably had more to leave than any of the Twelve. John Keble, in *The Christian Year*, thus beautifully celebrates the call of Matthew:

> At once he rose, and left his gold;
>     His treasure and his heart
> Transferred, where he shall safe behold
>     Earth and her idols part;
> While he beside his endless store
> Shall sit and floods unceasing pour
> Of Christ's true riches o'er all time and space,
> First angel of His Church, first steward of His grace!

It is significant that Mark and Luke in their account of the call of Matthew call him not Matthew, but Levi. The supposition is that when he became a disciple of Jesus, Matthew assumed a new name, like Peter and Paul, and that his new name was to him the sign and symbol of his new life.

Levi, the renegade Jew, the publican, the deserter, the traitor, the infamous one, was dead, and a new man, Matthew, the disciple of Jesus, had been born. All that he had done was a hole in which he had buried his past life and his old name.

Matthew is thus to be distinguished among the Twelve as the man in whom already Christ, before the period of training, had wrought a profound transformation. Peter, Andrew, James, John, Philip, and Nathanael were all earnest, devout Jews, perhaps all of them disciples of the great reformer, John the Baptist, when they became disciples of Jesus. That new relationship, when we consider their character and the nature of John's teaching, was a natural step in advance for them; it betokened spiritual growth rather than moral transformation and spiritual revolution.

But with Matthew it was different: he was, at least in public estimation, a sinner, an abandoned creature, a man past saving or helping, a traitor to all good things, the last man in the world to be interested in John or in Jesus. For him to leave the lucrative business of the tax collector and join himself to the wandering disciples of Jesus meant a profound moral change, a mighty upheaval in his soul. For this reason Matthew in his very call was a type of the moral transformation which Christ is able to effect in men's lives. By calling Matthew to follow him, Jesus showed that He was able to save even to the uttermost all them that come unto Him.

It took courage for Matthew to follow Christ, for this renegade Hebrew, this apostate Levite, this tool of the despised tax lords to go into the fellowship of men like Peter and James and John. But whatever the price was, Matthew paid it gladly. He succeeded not only in winning the confidence and friendship of the zealous Jews who were now his companions, but he lived to write the great Gospel in which he makes honorable amends for his erstwhile apostasy by showing how Jesus is the fulfiller of Old Testament prophecy, quoting the Old Testament sixty-five times and calling Jesus the Son of David eight times. Remember, when you are reading this Gospel, this most Hebrew of all the four, that it was written by Matthew, the faithful disciple of Jesus, but once Levi the son of Alphæus, the publican and apostate, the man who had sold his Levitical birthright for a mess of Roman pottage.

The only other incident in which Matthew figures in the Gospel narratives is that of the feast which he made for Jesus, the "great feast," as Luke terms it. Matthew modestly says that Jesus was sitting at meat in "the" house, but Mark and Luke tell us that the house was Matthew's (Mark 2:15; Luke 5:29). He meant it as an honor to his new Master, perhaps also as a sort of farewell to his old friends and associates, for "there was a great company of publicans and sinners and others." (Mark and Luke.)

It is possible to overdo the appeal of Christ to the poor and humble. He speaks to other classes as well, and here we have Him entertained at a costly banquet by His well-to-do disciple, Matthew. That was Matthew's natural way of showing respect to Jesus. He knew how to entertain, how to have a supper, a feast, and he made Jesus such an offering.

The presence of Jesus among the publicans scandalized the Scribes and Pharisees, who said to the disciples of Jesus, "How is it that He eateth and drinketh with publicans and sinners?" (Mark 2:16). Their exception gave Jesus opportunity for one of His most telling sentence sermons. Accepting, satirically of course, their estimate of themselves as righteous and of the publicans as sinners, He said, "They that are whole have no need of the physician, but they that are sick: I came not to call the righteous, but sinners to repentance." It was an overwhelming bit of irony. Then he changed His tone and said, "Go ye and learn what that meaneth, I will have mercy and not sacrifice," thereby implying that what the Pharisees and Scribes called righteousness was not acceptable to God.

Matthew, finally, put great value on the past. The great effort of his Gospel is to show that the life and ministry of Christ fulfilled the Scriptures and the prophecies. He does not begin to talk about Christ, about God, about religion in that tone which has become so popular in our day, as if the writer or speaker were the "first that ever burst" upon the silent sea of faith, as if he were a pioneer in religious thought and endeavor. The magnificent past, the words that God at sundry times and in divers manners spake in times past unto the Fathers, Matthew did not scorn, but treasured, and over them he pondered. He was not the man who would try to put a fool's cap upon all the past religious history of man, but made it a foundation upon which to stand, a giant's shoulder, as it were, from which he might look farther into the future and into the mysteries of God than those who stood merely upon the ground of their own experience.

Christianity assumes magnificent proportions when we take it with its splendid Old Testament background. It becomes a sublime plan, an unfolding panorama of God's power and grace, "even the mystery which hath been hid from ages and from generations, but now is made manifest to the saints: to whom God would make known what is the riches of the glory of this mystery among the Gentiles; which is Christ in you, the hope of glory." (Colossians 1:26, 27.)

# SIMON THE ZEALOT

take up the study of the disciple called Simon Zelotes imme-diately after that of Matthew the publican for the reason that they present such a contrast, and in their persons illustrate the catholicity of Jesus and the universality of His Church. Worldly prudence would have forbidden the selection of both Matthew and Simon —of Matthew because he was a hated publican, a renegade Jew, and an apostate Levite; of Simon because he erred on the other side, being a Zealot, that is, a member of the extreme revolutionary and radical party. The utmost concession that worldly prudence would have made would be to sanction the selection of one of these men, but not of both of them. Bad enough to have either type in a band of men that was to establish the spiritual throne of Israel, but still worse to have them both together in the same fellowship.

But Jesus showed at the very beginning that His kingdom was not of this world. None would have chosen as He chose; none would have built as He commenced to build. He took a detested publican and a fiery agitator into the same company of his disciples. The tax collector and the tax hater both followed Jesus.

In his article on Matthew Dr. John Kitto writes, "Few things are more suggestive to the thoughtful mind than the scantiness of our knowledge of the lives and actions of the apostles and evangelists of our Lord. Of several of the Twelve nothing beyond the names has reached us; others are barely mentioned in the Gospel narrative, and that chiefly in the way of blame or remonstrance. Of the very chiefest of them, the thing to be noted is not what we know but what we do not know. Of their work in the evangelism of the world little or nothing remains beyond vague traditions.''

We feel this scantiness of material when we come to speak of Simon, for we know nothing of him save that he was one of the Twelve and that he was called the Zealot, also the Canaanite —both names have a party significance. It is only his epithet that justifies us in venturing to speak of Simon. Most scholars agree that this epithet, ''the Zealot,'' ''connects Simon unmistakably with the famous party which rose in rebellion under Judas in the days of the taxing, some thirty years before Christ's ministry began, when Judæa and Samaria were brought under the direct government of Rome, and the census of the population was taken with a view to subsequent taxation.''

Gamaliel's speech before the council advising moderation in dealing with Peter and John, as recorded in Acts the fifth chapter, gives us the history of that insurrection: ''Ye men of Israel, take heed to yourselves what ye intend to do as touching these men. For before these days rose up Theudas, boasting himself to be somebody; to whom a number of men, about four hundred, joined themselves: who was slain; and all, as many as obeyed him, were scattered and brought to nought. After this man rose up Judas of Galilee, in the days of the taxing, and drew away much people after him: he also perished; and all, even as many as obeyed him, were dispersed.''

The fires of this insurrection still smouldered in the days of Jesus' ministry, and it is reasonable to think that Simon belonged to this party, a Hebrew Sinn Fein.

If the contrast between Simon and Matthew was great, still greater the contrast between Simon and Jesus. ''How singular a phenomenon,'' writes Alexander Bruce, ''is this ex-zealot among the disciples of Jesus. No two men could differ more widely in their spirit, ends and means than Judas of Galilee and Jesus of Nazareth. The one was a political malcontent; the other would have the conquered bow to the yoke and give to Cæsar Cæsar's due. The former aimed at restoring the kingdom of Israel, adopting for his watchword 'We have no Lord or Master but God'; the latter aimed at founding a kingdom, not national, but universal; not of this world, but purely spiritual. The means employed by the two actors were as diverse as their ends. One had recourse to the carnal weapons of war, the sword and the dagger; the other relied solely on the gentle but omnipotent force of truth'' (*The Training of the Twelve*, page 34).

I do not think that the fiery enthusiasm of Simon was permitted to burn itself out, but that now it burned to a better end, burned with devotion to Christ and to His universal empire. Like Peter, like John, like Paul, Simon, when he became a disciple of Jesus, was the same personality, the same character, but with a new aim and a new object for his powers.

It is true that the Church has suffered and does now suffer from the efforts of those who have zeal, but not according to knowledge. But if the Church has suffered from that kind of zeal, still more has it suffered from the lack of any kind of zeal. How many of us have any qualifications for repeating the words of the Psalmist which Jesus applied to Himself, "The zeal of Thine house hath eaten me up"?

> Holy Spirit, Truth Divine,
>   Dawn upon this soul of mine;
> Word of God, and inward Light,
>   Wake my spirit, clear my sight.
>
> Holy Spirit, Love Divine,
>   Glow within this heart of mine;
> Kindle every high desire;
>   Perish self in Thy pure fire!

The zeal of Simon poured itself forth in the form of patriotism. By a thrust of the sword, had it been possible, he would have restored the Kingdom of Israel. When he became an apostle his energies were directed towards the establishment of a greater kingdom. How long it was before Simon came to an understanding of what the kingdom meant we do not know. But we do know that at the very last Jesus 'disciples asked Him, "Wilt Thou at this time restore again the kingdom to Israel?" (Acts 1:6). Only the fires of Pentecost and the educative and expanding influences of their subsequent ministry let them know what Christ meant by the restoration of His kingdom and its unworldly nature.

But ideally, at least, the apostle and disciple of Jesus is a man who prays and strives for the coming of the kingdom of God. Simon is transformed from the Hebrew patriot to the Christian patriot. The change that was wrought in Him is one that is not easily accomplished. It was the work of the Holy Spirit.

The transformation remains the great need of the Church, of the Christian disciple, that he should become in regard to his faith denationalized and rise to the true dignity and responsibility of his citizenship in the kingdom—or better, commonwealth—which is heaven.

He must salute the day when all national anthems shall blend into one great chorus of the nations, people of every tribe and kindred and people and tongue, ascribing majesty and glory to the Lamb slain from the foundation of the world.

# JAMES THE LESS

The question of the identity of this James, whether or not he is James the brother of the Lord, the pillar of the Church, and the author of the epistle bearing the name of James, has been declared to be the most difficult in apostolic history. Indeed, there are very good reasons for identifying the son of Alphæus with the brother of the Lord, and also very good reasons for taking them as distinct, different individuals.

In the four catalogues of the Twelve as given in Matthew, Mark, Luke and the Acts, this second James is called the son of Alphæus, Mark in his account of the crucifixion calling him James the Less, or "little," either because of his low stature or because he was younger than James, the son of Zebedee.

One might take the epithet applied to James, "the less," and speak of the necessary part to be played by the undistinguished disciple. James, the Son of Thunder, was needed by Christ, but so was James the Less, the comparatively insignificant, whose sole history is in his name.

If this James is not the brother of the Lord, then we know nothing of him, as to his own characteristics, where he preached and how he witnessed. But from the testimony of Christ, we know that he kept the Word of God that Christ had committed unto them. Luke tells us that the son of Alphæus was with the apostolic band after the ascension, and we doubt not that he remained faithful to the end and did well his part in the building up of the walls of the Christian edifice.

Traveling much through the country one summer, I was impressed with the lasting service that had been rendered by the men of past generations who built the stone bridges over the creeks and rivers, well-rounded stone arches which still bear the burdens of traffic. They were gone, all these building hands, but their works remain. Who they were none knows. What they did, what they wrought, all know.

So thought Thomas Carlyle, looking one day over the bridge at Auldgarth: "A noble craft it is, that of a mason; a good building will last longer than most books, than one book in a million. The Auldgarth Bridge still spans the water silently, defies its chafing. There hangs it and will hang, grim and strong, when of all the cunning hands that piled it together, perhaps the last is now powerless in the sleep of death. O Time! O Time! wondrous and fearful art thou, yet there is in man what is above thee!"

Here, too, were leafy avenues of oak or elm or locust trees. The hands that planted the trees could hardly have profited by them, for the planters had gone to their graves by the white churches on the hilltops before the trees had come to maturity. It was a noble service rendered to the future, to the next generation. God makes use of man's own plans and ambitions and thereby man will unconsciously serve the tomorrow of humanity. But the highest form of human greatness has always seemed to me that effort which a man puts forth in his generation, knowing that he cannot profit by it, but that generations to come will profit. Of such is the race of tree planters. They sleep in unknown or unheeded graves, but the trees that they planted give shade to man and shelter to the birds of the air.

A veteran of the Civil War said to me several years ago, speaking of the world conflict then raging, "Everybody wants to be an officer in this war!" The indictment was too sweeping—not "everybody" by any means. But what he meant to say was that it struck him there were a great many of your young men who were thinking about the war more in terms of rank, of the grade they might hold or attain to, than of the great service they might render to humanity. I once heard the relatives of a New England man bitterly assailing the government because he had not been appointed to the rank for which they thought him fitted. The fact that a great cause was being served and that, after all, the service of a private in the ranks, giving his life if need be, was, in such a cause, all that a noble soul could ask—that seemed entirely to have escaped them. But the casualty lists told the tale. The private soldier won the crown of glory in the Great War, as in that other conflict of liberty sixty years ago.

In that ancient battle against the Amalekites, when David smote them in revenge for the sack of Ziklag, the three hundred men who were told to abide by the stuff, to guard the camp, shared equally in the spoils of battle with the others whose swords were red with the blood of the invaders. "As his part is that goeth down to the battle, so shall his part be that tarrieth by the stuff: they shall part alike" (1 Sam. 30:24).

That old law of David was a reflection of the Divine Law. God needs James the Son of Thunder, James the first martyr among the Twelve, but He needs as well James the Less, concerning whom no fact, save his name and his apostolic rank, has been preserved in the files of history. "They also serve who only stand and wait."

I am not convinced that this James was not the brother of the Lord, and one reason for thinking that he was is the remarkable number of similes and metaphors drawn from nature which appear in the Epistle of James and which bear a marked resemblance to those which were employed by Jesus in His teaching. A brother of the Lord would be familiar with that teaching. But if he is not, and if we know nothing of James but his name and those of his father and mother, and regardless of whether the epithet "the Less" refers only to stature or years and not to importance—still in his history and service as an apostle of the Lord Jesus Christ we have an example of a pure and altogether unselfish service for Christ.

That is what will make good workmen of us all, to be impressed with the majesty of Jesus, the supremacy of the Kingdom of God, and the eternal worth of contributing our share to the advancement of that Kingdom.

The gleaming stones of the cemeteries on the hilltops, the abounding instances of shattered plans and baffled ambitions, the unsatisfactoriness of that which man has at length secured after long struggle, the poor relics of men who dreamed and toiled and wrought all about us—all this would be of a nature to cast a shadow over life and make man seriously ask himself the question, "Is it worth while?"

The Apostle Paul knew that the disciples at Corinth, living in a world of vicissitude and change, perplexed and troubled, their society preyed upon by death not less remorselessly than the society of the Christless, could not help asking themselves that old question about the use of trying to live as followers of Christ, of laboring and suffering for Him. His answer for them came with a mighty reassurance at the end of the sublime argument for immortality in the first letter to the Corinthians: "Therefore, my beloved brethren, be ye steadfast, unmovable, always abounding in the work of the Lord, forasmuch as ye know that your labor is not in vain in the Lord."

That is the Christian's ground and hope. Because of Christ, because of the light He has poured into life, because of the greatness of the Kingdom which He represents, they who live and toil in faith in Him cannot live and cannot toil in vain. Our labor is not in vain in the Lord. Yes, that is our goal, to labor, to stand by the truth in Christ, to be loyal to the Church, to the pastor, to God's work, to Christian service. It is the work that "pays," if I may borrow a phrase from the market place. It pays in time, and in ways beyond our thinking and our dreaming, it will pay in eternity.

# PHILIP

Philip does not scintillate. He makes no great blunders, neither does he attract attention by striking deeds or brilliant sayings. To me he is the common, everyday Christian, following his Master faithfully; no son of thunder, either for good or for evil; not always seeing the reason for things as they come and go; a little dull at times in catching the meaning of the words and acts of Christ, but nevertheless continuing in His steps; an average two-talent sort of Christian, and therefore, perhaps, more than any of the Twelve representative of those who were to believe on the Name of Jesus.

Because of his Greek name and the fact that it was to him first of all that the enquiring Greeks came when they desired to see Jesus, it has been thought that Philip had Greek connections. This is possible. Or it may have been just by accident that the Greeks happened to come upon Philip first among the disciples. But, whether by choice or by accident, their first approaching Philip was a fortunate event. He was a man who would hear carefully what they had to say and take time for a decision.

I can imagine that if the Greeks had come first to the Sons of Thunder, John or James, or even Peter, they would have told them to be gone, that Jesus had nothing to say to Greeks or other Gentiles, but only to the children of Abraham. But when they say to Philip, "We would see Jesus," they come upon a man who receives them kindly and, if not making a decision himself, sees that their cause has a fair hearing.

Philip took Greeks to Andrew, evidently counting on his sympathy and on his sound advice, and then Philip and Andrew took them to Jesus. This first appeal from the world outside of Israel stirred our Saviour to the depths of His being. In these enquiring, reverent Greeks He saw the prophecy of the great host that would come to follow Him and believe on His Name, finding in Him the Way, the Truth, and the Life. He beheld the long procession of saints and martyrs coming from the east and the west, the north and the south. What wonder that He exclaimed, "Father, glorify Thy Name!"

In Philip, then, we have a man who, in the small band of disciples, himself an Hebrew, was nevertheless an approachable man not out of touch or sympathy with the world that differed from his own. He was not a Christian who had become "churchified" so as to lose all touch with men without the Church, unable to meet with them or talk with them. We believe that Jesus is the only Way, Truth, and Life, and we know that the light of natural religion is not enough to guide a man to salvation, else had Christ not died. Yet we like to think that always "other sheep not of this fold" belong to Christ and that in ways unknown to you and me Christ draws them unto Himself.

It was also Philip who, at the Last Supper, asked one of the questions which elicited from Jesus some memorable answers. Jesus had said, "Whither I go ye know and the way ye know." That moved Thomas to exclaim, "Lord, we know not whither Thou goest, and how can we know the way?" To this Jesus replied, "I am the Way, the Truth and the Life. No man cometh unto the Father but by Me. If ye had known Me, ye should have known My Father also." Then Philip asked the question that so often lies unspoken in our minds, that question which underlies all religion — no dull, stupid question as is so often thought, but the great fundamental question — "Lord, show us the Father and it sufficeth us!"

For years now Philip had heard Jesus speak of God as His Father, and of how He had come to do the Father's will, and how He and the Father were one. Philip was perplexed by the relationship, as many a Christian since has been, and he thought he would clear the whole atmosphere by this question about God.

Whatever he was or was not, Philip knew how to ask a great question. It is no common gift. Some men can teach more by questions than others can by declarations or answers. Who was this Father? Where was He? How would He appear? Show me the Father! How often, how often, looking at night up into the starry heavens, so calm, so luminous, so glorious, we have asked ourselves, "Where is He that made them? Why does He hide Himself so wondrously as if there were no God at all?" Or, in the midst of great waters, all the billows of fate and disaster sweeping over the soul, we have asked the same question, "Lord, who art Thou that runnest upon me? Where art Thou? Why art Thou far from helping me, O my God?" Jesus, who was made in all things like unto His brethren, uttered the same cry, passed through that same gulf of temporary yearning and uncertainty about God. "And about the ninth hour Jesus cried with a loud voice saying, *Eloi, Eloi, lama sabachthani?* which is, being interpreted, My God, My God, why hast Thou forsaken Me?" A God who has forsaken us is a God who is not.

Yes, could we but interpret many a cry and many a prayer that is wrung from human lips, of all races, creeds and tongues, we should find, I think, that, being interpreted in the language universal of the soul, it means this: "Why hast Thou forsaken me? Where is God? Who is God?" To hold to our faith in God, that is where the battle of life is won or lost.

Jesus Christ is the answer to humanity's cry. More than we think it, judging by those who resort to houses of prayer and worship, men in some way ask themselves Philip's great question about God. That man must trouble himself with such a question—that, made in God's image, he must yet wonder if there is a God and how God works and what He is—is one of the sad results of sin. Something dreadful has happened: man's natural and easy fellowship with God has been broken, broken by human sin, and thus it is that Christ, taking upon Himself our nature and bearing our sins, had, when He was dying on the Cross, that same experience of the broken fellowship; God drifted from Him. "My God, why hast Thou forsaken Me?" But He was forsaken that we might never be forsaken.

Still He walks among men, into the dark house of sorrow, through the corridors of pain in the hospital, amid the debris and human wreckage of the awful battlefields where men like beasts have fought with beasts, and with infinite compassion and tenderness answers all these cries, saying, "He that hath seen Me hath seen the Father."

With that great saying, and without discussing the relationship existing between the members of the adorable Trinity, Father, Son and Holy Ghost, let us comfort our hearts. We know that Christ has come; that Jesus lived and died and rose again; that His words are before us. Whatever this world may seem to say of God, stars, seas, wind-bowed forests, tragedies in nature and in man's life, losses, griefs, shipwrecks, hurricanes, whirlwinds of misfortune and disaster, let us remember that the final and authoritative word about God, as Father and Redeemer, is Jesus Christ.

I end these meditations upon Philip by going back to the beginning. "The day following Jesus would go forth into Galilee, and findeth Philip, and saith unto him, Follow Me. Now Philip was of Bethsaida, the city of Andrew and Peter. Philip findeth Nathanael, and saith unto him, We have found Him, of whom Moses in the law and the prophets did write, Jesus of Nazareth, the son of Joseph. And Nathanael said unto him, Can there any good thing come out of Nazareth?" Nathanael was a very thoughtful, probably mentally trained man and philosopher. He thinks it absurd that the Messiah should be found in Nazareth. Perhaps that expression of prejudice was intended only as the introductory remarks to a long discussion about the Messiah, when and where He should make His appearance.

But Philip, who was no logician, no philosopher, only a plain man with a great deal of common sense, interrupted all Nathanael's learned discussion by saying, "Come and see." He did not get angry with Nathanael for doubting his judgment, nor did he debate with him the matter. He simply said, "Come and see."

Christ likes that test. Some men may have a reputation for wisdom or piety, but would shrink from examination on these points. Christ welcomes the test. "Come and see." It is the best reason we can give when we ask anyone to believe on Jesus. More than that, it is an invitation that ofttimes we must extend to ourselves, to our own doubting hearts or rebellious will, "Come and see." Come and see if He is not the Fountain of Life. Come and see if He is not able to restore and forgive. "O taste and see that the Lord is good. Blessed is the man that trusteth in Him."

# JUDAS WHO BETRAYED HIM

And as to Judas Iscariot, my reason is different. I would fain see the face of him who, having dipped his hand in the same dish with the Son of Man, could afterwards betray Him. I have no conception of such a thing; nor have I ever seen any picture (not even Leonardo's very fine one) that gave me the least idea of it.'' So, according to William Hazlitt in his essay on *Persons One Would Wish to Have Seen*, spake Charles Lamb. And so say we all. Could we see his face we might get some idea of the man and some understanding of his crime.

Judas is the man of mystery among the Twelve. "I have no conception of such a thing," said Lamb, meaning of a man who could dip his hand in the same dish with Jesus and then betray Him. Judas is the most definitely classified disciple among the Twelve; "who betrayed Him" is the epithet of infamy with which the Gospels hand him down to succeeding generations. Yet how hard it is to conceive of Judas, his call to the discipleship, his treason, his remorse, his fearful taking-off. The end and the beginning in him perplex and baffle us.

When we come to study him we confront the mystery of predestination and man's free will, easily scoffed at and ridiculed, or conveniently dismissed, but in the life of Judas a fact to be reckoned with, if indeed, there is any fact presented to us by the Four Gospels. Here, too, we are confronted by the mystery of the Satanic element in human nature, the evil, diabolical possibilities of the soul of man. "One of you is a devil," said Jesus. And yet He had chosen him. "Satan entered him," wrote John. Yet Judas broke his heart and his body with remorse for his sin against the Son of God.

It is this mystery of human nature that we feel when we take up the character of Judas Iscariot, the mystery of evil, primarily, but also the mystery of good, for although Judas died by his own hand in a fit of despair, that despair was the fruit of remorse. If the crime of Judas perplexes us—how a man could do it, betray Jesus with a kiss, and for twenty dollars—still more does his remorse perplex us. A man, according to all experience, who could commit such an abnormal crime ought to have been too bad a man to suffer such a remorse. If, on the one hand, it seems that such a crime is beyond the possibility of human nature, so, on the other hand, granted that a man could be found to commit the crime, it seems that such a criminal ought to be beyond all reach of sorrow or remorse. There is Judas: so vile that he can dip his hand with Christ in the dish and then go out and betray Him; yet so sorry for his crime that he goes out and hangs himself.

Having mentioned in this way the remorse of Judas, I now consider for a moment those analyses of Judas' crime which make it not a crime at all. Undoubtedly, the record of the remorse of Judas has been the fountain whence these theories or explanations have flowed. Since it is difficult to reconcile the remorse of Judas with his transgression, efforts have been made to seek for motives other than those which the Scriptures attribute to Judas, or rather hint at, for it is highly significant that the Gospels merely state that Judas was a traitor, that he betrayed Him, they do not say why he betrayed Him.

One such hypothesis is that Judas was not a traitor in the sense that he sought to compass the death of Jesus. The foundation stone of this theory is that Judas, in common with all the disciples, was looking forward to the establishment of a Messianic kingdom by Jesus in which he would have one of the twelve thrones that Jesus had promised to His disciples. He was disappointed that Jesus refused to let the people in Galilee make Him a king (John 6:15), and became more and more impatient as Jesus postponed from day to day the setting up of the Kingdom. Jesus himself had accepted the title of Messiah from the Twelve (Matthew 16:16). Why, then, did He not assume the splendor and take the throne of the Messiah?

Judas at length resolves to force such a step on the part of Christ. He plans to precipitate the crisis by bringing Jesus face to face with his adversaries. To accomplish this before the crowds which were attending the passover had left Jerusalem and dispersed to their own towns and villages, Judas resolves to go through an act of seeming desertion and treason. He will play the part of a traitor and precipitate the crisis between Jesus and those who oppose Him. In that crisis Christ would declare His Messiahship and set up His throne.

Judas counted upon forgiveness and restoration and a share in the glory of the kingdom as soon as Jesus understood his action. Because he believed that Jesus was the Messiah he knew He could not die (John 12:34), and even when he had betrayed Him with a kiss in the garden he heard Jesus say that twelve legions of angels were at His command.

But Judas had made a miscalculation. Jesus did acknowledge Himself as the Messiah, yet, what was unthinkable to Judas, and now filled him with dismay and horror, He permitted Himself to be condemned to death. Judas hurried to the priests and tried to make a last desperate effort to undo the sad matter, and failing in this, overwhelmed with remorse and despair, hanged himself.

According to this hypothesis, Judas, for the sake of worldly gain and glory, took great liberties with the person of Jesus, and was led on by consuming avarice, but he was not guilty of wilfully contriving the death of Jesus—that is, at heart he was no traitor. In the words of Archbishop Whately, "the difference between Iscariot and his fellow-apostles was that, though they all had the same expectations and conjectures, he dared to act on his conjectures, departing from the plain course of his known duty to follow the calculation of his worldly wisdom and the schemes of his worldly ambition" (*Discourse on the Treason of Judas Iscariot and Notes*).

Thomas De Quincey, in his entertaining essay on Judas, travels over much the same course as that taken by Archbishop Whately, but goes far beyond him. The Archbishop relieved Judas of the odium of treason, of betraying his Friend and Master, but leaves him with the condemnation of colossal covetousness and worldly ambition resting upon him. But De Quincey lifts Judas to the pinnacle of mistaken but sincere and sacrificial zeal for Christ's cause.

Here we have a man who willingly takes upon himself the odium and infamy of the traitor, knowing that the Scriptures must be fulfilled, that someone must play the part of a traitor before Jesus asserts His royal powers and takes His throne and reigns. This Judas is no traitor, but the prince of the martyrs. His only mistake was a mistake of judgment, not of love, not of faith, not of avarice. When he saw that he had played the traitor in vain, then his heart broke with remorse and he hanged himself. In De Quincey's own words:

> To burst in the middle is simply to be shattered and ruined in the central organ of our sensibilities, which is the heart; and in saying that the viscera of Iscariot, or his middle, had burst and gushed out, the original reporter meant simply that his heart had broken. That was precisely his case. Out of pure anguish that the schemes which he meant for the sudden glorification of his Master had recoiled (according to all worldly interpretation) in his utter ruin; that the sudden revolution, through a democratic movement, which was to raise himself and his brother apostles into Hebrew princes, had scattered them like sheep without a shepherd; and that, superadded to this common burden of ruin, he personally had to bear a separate load of conscious disobedience to God and insupportable responsibility; naturally enough, out of all this, he fell into fierce despair; his heart broke, and under that storm of affliction he hanged himself.

Unfortunately, this is not the Judas of the Four Gospels. The only source that we have for knowledge that there was a Judas tells us that Judas was a traitor. No scheming politician, hoping to profit by the establishment of the Messianic kingdom; no heroic martyr, taking the part of a traitor in order to fulfill the Scriptures, but one who sold the Son of God for thirty pieces of silver and went to "his own place." The fourth evangelist and St. Luke speak of him and his crime with a shudder, "Satan entered into him."

The first question that we ask about Judas is: How did such a man come to be a member of the Twelve? What place had the son of perdition among the disciples of the Son of Man? That the Scriptures might be fulfilled, that the Son of Man might go as it had been written of Him (Matthew 26:24)? Life has too much deep tragedy in it, too many instances of members of the same apostolic band, the same family, the same class, the objects of the same father's prayers, those who kneeled at the same mother's knee—going some of them to the light, to honor, to faith, hope and love and good works, and some of them to the dark, to shame, to infamy, to violation of the laws of God and of man—going, like Judas, out into the blackest night, alone, forever alone—for anyone to dismiss with a smile what God's Word teaches us about the eternal decrees and purposes of God. This mystery has been touched upon by Oliver Wendell Holmes in his *Two Streams*:

Behold the rocky wall
That down its sloping sides
Pours the swift raindrops, blending as they fall,
In rushing river-tides!

Yon stream, whose sources run
Turned by a pebble's edge,
Is Athabasca, rolling toward the sun
Through the cleft mountain-ledge.

The slender rill had strayed,
But for the slanting stone,
To evening's ocean, with the tangled braid
Of foam-flecked Oregon.

So from the heights of Will
Life's parting stream descends,
And, as a moment turns its slender rill,
Each widening torrent bends,

From the same cradle's side,
From the same mother's knee,
One to long darkness and the frozen tide,
One to the Peaceful Sea!

In more telling language it has been dealt with by Rossetti in his *Jenny*:

Just as another woman sleeps!
Enough to throw one's thoughts in heaps
Of doubt and horror—what to say
Or think—this awful secret sway,
The potter's power over the clay!
Of the same lump (it has been said)
For honor and dishonor made,
Two sister vessels. Here is one.

We can neither add to nor take from the words of Scripture concerning this mystery, and there, in humble awe, knowing that the Judge of all earth must do right, we leave it. But we can speak of Judas on the side of his own will, his own decrees, his own place. We cannot think either that he was chosen to play the part of the traitor as a stage manager might choose an actor to take the villain's part in a play, or that Judas joined the cause of Christ with purposes of treachery in his heart, or even with unworthy mercenary motives. As we have seen, all the disciples hoped to gain something by the surrender they had made to Christ. Christ himself seemed to countenance such hopes. When Peter said, ''Lo, we have left all, and have followed Thee,'' Jesus responded that His disciples would receive ''an hundredfold *now in this time*, houses, and brethren, and sisters'' (Mark 10:28-30).

What were his motives? Very likely Judas was as sincere in his motives and as worthy or unworthy as the rest of the disciples. He had good in him and evil, but while contact with Christ drew out the good and banished the evil in the other disciples, with Judas the reverse seems to have been the case. With him Christ was a savor of death unto death.

Avarice undoubtedly played its part in his downfall. If so, how telling the words of Jesus about laying up treasure in heaven! John says plainly that he was a thief and pilfered from the bag. His thieving instinct made him blow with his tainted breath upon the beautiful offering of Mary to Jesus, complaining that the money might have been given to the poor. But once in the bag, Judas, and not the poor, would have profited by the sum. Leonardo takes him in the moment of the question at the table, ''Lord, is it I?'' There he sits, furtive-browed and dark-visaged, clutching the bag with an eager right hand.

It has been objected that if avarice were a motive in the crime, Judas should have profited more by continued stealings from the treasury, whereas the act of treachery brought him but twenty dollars and put an end to all further gain. But it is best to be guided here not by what other men might have done under similar circumstances, but by what Judas did. He sold Him for thirty pieces of silver. If avarice played its part in the breakdown of the character of Judas, it is nothing strange or unheard of.

Men with visions of the truth and with a supply of good motives have been brought to disastrous ends through love of filthy lucre. Witness the gifted Balaam, Numbers 22-24, who could wish he were of the number of Israel and could die the death of the righteous Hebrew, yet for gold is eager to curse them. Those two men, the admiring, truth-desiring, peace-seeking man, and the other money-loving, good-hating man, resided in the heart of Balaam and in the heart of Judas, and, alas! in the heart of many a man since. For the sake of money, and what money can bring, ''just for a piece of silver,'' men have deserted noble causes and played false that great cause of truth and righteousness which, once at least in every man's life, calls upon him to serve her.

That Judas was shocked at the pretensions of Jesus, at His making Himself co-equal with God, at His fierce denunciations of the ruling classes at Jerusalem, and was actuated by patriotic motives in deserting Jesus, or that he was jealous of the Galilean disciples, he himself being the only Judæan, we dismiss as pure imagination and contrary to the record, the only record we have.

There are, however, not wanting evidences that vindictiveness and revenge entered into his crime, as well as avarice. We must try to account for the hate that Judas bore to Jesus leading him to such a step. It is no uncommon experience that the darkness hateth the light. Judas knew that Jesus knew from the beginning that he was a traitor, or had treasonable propensities. Once He said that one of His disciples had a devil. Judas knew whom He meant. Jesus warned and reproved him, but these warnings, instead of recalling him and making him bring forth the fruits of repentance, sent him farther along the path of crime.

It is significant that both Matthew and Mark say it was after Jesus had rebuked him for interfering with Mary's gift of precious ointment that Judas began to seek opportunity to betray Him. The devil of vengeance began to brood in the heart of Judas. This helps us to understand the kiss in the Garden. The leaders of the band knew Jesus, it was not necessary that He should be so identified. But to a vindictive, revenge-seeking spirit, the darkest, cruelest spirit that can take hold of man or woman, how sweet that kiss in the Garden! God save us from the soul-destroying monster of sin in the form of hate or vindictiveness.

When Judas had received the sop at that Last Supper, two things happened: Jesus said to him, "That thou doest, do quickly;" and Satan entered into him. The words of Jesus and the receiving of the sop marked the crisis in the soul of Judas. Now there was no further delaying, no longer halting between two opinions, no longer playing the part of a traitor and yet remaining a disciple. The hour had come when Judas had to choose between good and evil, between Christ and gold, between the light and darkness.

Judas chose the dark, the night, and immediately Satan, who had entered into him before only by way of suggestion and temptation, now entered in to possess his own. The words of Jesus, the last save the exclamation in the Garden that Jesus ever addressed to Judas, "That thou doest, do quickly!"

may be taken as a last warning, perhaps a last appeal. Which would Judas do, betray Him or be faithful to Him?

There have been worse men than Judas, for men who have been guilty of sin like his, who at least have done it unto "one of the least of these" and, therefore, unto Christ (Matthew 25:31-46), have yet not taken it to heart as Judas did. However infamous his sin, let us give Judas credit for a corresponding remorse. "Then Judas, which had betrayed Him, when he saw that He was condemned, repented himself and brought again the thirty pieces of silver to the chief priests and elders, saying, I have sinned, in that I have betrayed the innocent blood!" Now we begin to pity him.

Yes, every wrong-doer comes at length to that place where men and angels must pity him, where the wrong-doer himself must pity his ruined self. Judas had sold himself.

> Still as of old,
>     Man by himself is priced,
> For thirty pieces Judas sold
>     Himself, not Christ.

However we may analyse the motives of Judas, his career and his end dispose effectually of the very popular "moral environment theory," that good surroundings invariably make good men, and that bad men are just the natural result of bad surroundings. None could have had better surroundings than Judas had for three years. He walked and he talked with Christ, with Him who is the Way, the Truth, and the Life. Yet look at his end! Ah, in evil there are greater mysteries than the accidents of birth and place and station. The right kind of surroundings will help a man if he in his heart so wills it, but if his heart wills it not, then heaven itself would not keep him from going to destruction. It is possible to be near to Christ, to be in His Church, to sit at His table as Judas did, and yet be far from Him.

# PAUL

On a March afternoon in the year of salvation sixty, a gang of prisoners under the custody of a Roman centurion is descending the western slope of the Alban Hills. Each prisoner is chained to a soldier. This one is a man-stealer from Alexandria, this one a robber from Tyre, this one a murderer from Cæsarea, this one a rebel from Jerusalem. All look the part save this last prisoner, who is a Hebrew who has appealed to the jurisdiction of Cæsar, and is being taken to Rome to stand before Cæsar's judgment seat.

The Appian Way leads them across the vast spaces of the Roman campagna, now brilliant with the flowers of springtime. Now they are passing over the plain which, at a day not far distant, will be honeycombed with narrow subterranean passages, where men will lay their dead in hope of the doctrine of the resurrection which fell from the lips of the Jewish prisoner.

As they come nearer to the city, the road is filled with throngs of people, coming and going—farmers returning with empty carts from the market, cohorts of soldiers starting for the distant east or coming home after service in Africa, Greece or Asia, wealthy men carried in litters by slaves on their way to their summer villas on the hills, the chariots of generals and senators and proconsuls. To Julius and his band of prisoners all these give hardly a glance as they pass.

Now the prisoners pass by the colossal tombs of the great men of Rome, then at length into the city, past temples, statues, arches, baths, colonnades, and palaces, whose gilded roofs flash back the afternoon sun—down into the Forum and up the Capitoline Hill to the barracks of the Prætorian Guard, where Julius hands over his prisoners.

The dream of one of these prisoners has come true! He has come to Rome!

Yet, save among a few obscure believers, his entry excited not a ripple of interest or comment. Rome's greatest conqueror entered her gates that day. When the proud monuments of imperial splendor upon which this prisoner gazed as he passed through the city shall have been leveled with the dust and under the dust, Rome's most conspicuous monument will be a temple dedicated to the faith of that lonely prisoner.

It is not my purpose to speak of Paul's place in history. That place is forever secure. He needs no explanation and no defense. What I wish to do rather is to say something of the man who did these mighty works, the messenger who carried the message which turned the world upside down, the lamp which bore the light which lighted the darkness of this world.

Paul once asked the Corinthians to be followers of him as he was of Christ. Who could imitate Paul, the versatility of his genius, his great experience with Christ, the power and cogency of his thought, and the eloquence of his tongue? Yet there is much in him which is capable of imitation and where humble Christians can follow him. Of that let us now speak.

*First*, his appreciation of the dignity of human nature. This is always a mark of a great soul. Paul showed his high thought of the worth and dignity of man by a high regard for himself. I have always counted it a fortunate thing that he who is the great teacher as to the sinfulness of man and the corruption of human nature was no mealy-mouthed weakling, but the manliest man that ever lived.

We have an instance of this in Paul's reply to the Roman officers at Philippi, who, when they discovered that they had scourged and imprisoned without trial a Roman citizen, sent down messengers asking Paul to withdraw quietly from the city. But Paul answered in all the splendor of his self-respect, "They have beaten us openly, uncondemned, being Romans, and they cast us into prison: and now do they thrust us out privily? Nay, verily: but let them come themselves and fetch us out."

We have another echo of this in his rebuke of the high priest who, at the trial of Paul before the Sanhedrin, commanded the soldier to smite Paul on the mouth. Instantly Paul scorched him with the flame of his righteous indignation: "God shall smite thee, thou whited wall, for sittest thou to judge me after the law and commandest me to be smitten contrary to the law?" It was a ringing testimony to the rights of man.

Paul was able to respect himself because, he tells us, he always lived so as to have a conscience void of offense toward God and man. If Paul was a chosen vessel, let it be remembered that he was also a clean vessel before he was chosen. The first factor in any good and useful life is the respect of self. The man who does not live so as to have his own self-respect cannot hope to reach or touch other men.

*Second*, his love for man. He who had such high thoughts of the worth and dignity of human nature was a fit vessel to bear to the world the doctrines of the Gospel which affirmed the worth of every soul and a noble destiny through faith in Christ.

Yet this love for men was not a natural gift with Paul. Of all men, at the outset, he would seem the least qualified to become the bearer of the tidings that God had made of one blood all nations of men. He appears in the theater of human action as a man possessed by the fiercest prejudices and antipathies, as an intense nationalist of the narrowest sect, seeing nothing good beyond the confines of Israel.

Yet this man, through the touch of Christ, becomes the apostle to the Gentiles, the first preacher of the doctrine of a nation of humanity, which is above all other nations. His traveling band, made up of Timothy, half Greek and Hebrew, Luke the Greek, Aristarchus and Sopater who were Macedonians, and Trophimus who was an Asiatic, was the first society of internationalists the world had ever seen.

When Paul died, his arms were stretched as wide apart as those of Christ upon the cross. In Chrysostom's eloquent words, "The dust of that heart which a man would not do wrong to call the heart of the world, so enlarged that it could take in cities, and nations, and peoples." The "desperate tides" of the whole world's anguish was forced through the channels of a single heart. "Who is weak and I am not weak? Who is made to stumble and I burn not?" He was debtor to all men, all races, all classes, all colors. Wherever a man breathed, wherever a heart beat, wherever a soul was enshrined, there was Paul with all his burning earnestness and yearning love. He was able to think nothing alien to himself.

When John Howard, the prisoner-reformer, died in a Russian lazzaretto, they put on his grave these words: "Reader, whosoever thou art, know that thou standest by the grave of a friend." Did we know where rests the dust of Paul, we could write like words over his tomb: "Reader, whosoever thou art, bond or free, Greek or barbarian, Jew or Gentile, black or white, red or yellow, man of the first, fifteenth or twentieth century, know that thou standest by the grave of a friend."

*Third*, the heroic element in the life of Paul. In our day there is a tendency to think that the heroism of the Christian life is to be found apart from great Christian beliefs and convictions. It is, therefore, a fact worthy of pause and reflection that it is the man of the deepest and most clearly outlined beliefs and doctrines who is also the noblest of the Christian heroes, as Chrysostom called him, "the wrestler for Christ."

We do not know a man until we have seen how he performs on the lonely platform of adversity, how he will act with the wind in his face. If there was ever a man born for adversity, and who inspires his fellow-men to take arms against a sea of troubles and by opposing end them, that man was St. Paul. It was no rhetoric, no mere figure of speech, when he spoke of bearing in his body the marks of the Lord Jesus Christ. What a catalogue of woes he mentions—thorns in the flesh and sicknesses of the body; through adversaries of the civil government, beatings and imprisonment; the frenzy of the mobs, who stoned him and clamored for his blood; the oath-bound assassins who dogged his tracks; the perils of the natural world, by sea, by river, in wilderness, and on mountaintop; the desertion and suspicion of his friends and cruel slander which, like a viper, has rustled in the withered leaves of dry and fallen hearts since the world began.

Heroic battler, noble wrestler for Christ! How many were thine adversaries! Was there a peril of sky or earth or sea that thou didst not face? Was there a wicked passion in the heart of man which did not select thee for its victim? Was there a cup of bitterness which thou didst not taste? Was there a thorn to which the flesh is heir that thou didst not endure? Yet in all things he was more than conqueror.

It is here that all of us become deeply interested in Paul. We all must face life, and, if it can be done triumphantly, we want to know how. In Paul's triumph there were at least three elements:

℄ His aim and purposes did not end with self. If his own pleasure and comfort and personal success had been his aim, then what a bitter disappointment life must have been to Paul! But he had scorn for those miserable aims which end with self. Personal defeats and overthrows did not shake his soul. Those personal vicissitudes which shock and overcome so many men were but minor incidents to this man, whose mind was set on a higher goal than self.

℄ God had a purpose to work out in his life. Whatever, therefore, the hard experience through which he had to pass, he could look under it and beyond it and back of it to the will and purpose of God. Things did not "happen" to Paul. The man who gives us the sublime and difficult doctrine about the sovereign decree of Almighty God, is also the man who gives us the incomparable demonstration of how that faith works in everyday life. He not only said it, but found it to be true, that sentence imbedded like a lovely crystal in the dark rock of the great chapter on predestination, "All things work together for good to them that love God."

℄ His fellowship with Christ was so close that he could make bold to say that Christ suffered in him.

Scotland has given many martyrs to the Church and to civil liberty, but there is no tale of martyrdom which so touches a Scottish heart as that of the two Wigtown martyrs, Mary and Agnes Wilson, who perished in the Solway tide. The elder sister was fastened to a stake much farther out than the younger, with the thought that when the younger saw the sufferings and death struggles of her sister she would recant. Quickly the inexorable tide of the Solway came in, first to the ankles, then to the knees, then to the waist, then to the neck, then to the lips. The executioners called to the younger sister, "Look! What seest thou?" Turning her head a little she saw the struggles of her drowning sister, and then made her calm answer, "What do I see? I see the Lord Jesus suffering in one of His members!"

In the darkest and most critical hours of his life St. Paul was conscious of the presence and the help of Christ —"But the Lord stood by me."

*Fourth*, the friendships of St. Paul. His was a heart which burned for everyone who was lost and was broken down by a brother's tears. Even if we did not have so many recorded instances of the deeply affectionate nature of St. Paul, we should know him to be that sort of man, for back of every great and good and lasting work there beats somewhere a warm and tender heart.

Napoleon at St. Helena wondered if in all the world a single person loved him. But to do justice to the friendships of St. Paul would require the tongue, not of man, but of an angel. In his letters come first the doctrines, then the practical precepts, and last the personal greetings—to Onesiphorus, who was not ashamed of his chains; to Epaphroditus, who came to minister to him in Rome and whom Paul nursed back to life; to Amplias, Narcissus, Herodian, Julia, Olympas, Rufus and "his mother and mine"; and then that last urgent message for best loved Timothy to come "before winter."

He who could smite with a Titan's fist the stronghold of Satan knew also how to lay a forget-me-not on the breast of a living friend or upon the grave of the dead. The thought of those friends whom he had made for himself and for Christ, "hearts he had won of sister or of brother, friends in the blameless family of God," the thought of these friends, the remembrance that they prayed for him, came like gleams of sunlight into the damp and gloom of that Mamertine dungeon at Rome. Salute! Salute! Salute! is his word as they lead him out to die. And thus with messages for those whose names he had written in the Lamb's Book of Life, Paul fades from this world into that other world where friends meet and aye are fair and where partings are no more.

All these friendships were summed up in the great and eternal friendship with Christ. That is why Paul's life is the greatest love story ever written. Love carried him over the blazing plains and miasmic marshes; love led him through the ghettos of the great Roman cities; love was the star by which he steered his course through the stormy Ægean and Mediterranean.

If I were asked to sum up his theology, his doctrine, I would not mention his great fundamental teachings as to the fall of man and the sinfulness that requires redemption; nor his profound statement as to the sovereign purposes of God's grace; nor his logical setting forth of the doctrine of justification by faith. I would sum it up in one single sentence, that sentence which must sum up all genuine Christianity, all true saving relationship with Christ: "I live by the faith of the Son of God, who loved me and gave Himself for me."

That mighty life is but the echo of that sentence which takes in the length and the depth and the breadth and the height of our faith, "He loved me and gave Himself for me." Forever true! As true of you as it was of Paul, or John. Christ loved you and gave Himself for you. But have you consented to that fact? Have you bowed down before it? Can you say it as Paul said it, "He loved me and gave Himself for me"?

> Christ! I am Christ's, and let the name suffice you,
>   Yea, for me too He greatly hath sufficed;
> Lo, with no winning word I would entice you,
>   Paul has no honor and no friend but Christ!

# An Epilogue

Thirteen photographs of portrait quality decorate the pages of this book. That much you already know. But who are the men behind the beards impersonating the Apostles? How did a truck driver, a barber, a cardiologist, and a disabled war veteran find their way into a studio and in front of a camera lens in order to pose as one of Christ's disciples?

There were no auditions, no advertisements, no special plans of selection at the outset of this project. There was a man with a camera who had a dream—that dream was to bring a sense of reality to Christianity by picturing real people in the roles of some of the Bible's characters. And there was God, the One who really directed the project.

The idea came in 1964. One year later I photographed my first "Apostle." He was a fellow Rotarian. Having returned from a vacation with a beautiful beard, I asked him to stop by the studio and pose as one of the early Christians. We didn't have a cloak for him to wear. We didn't even know which disciple he would be. A local tailor solved the first problem, and a viewing of the proofs solved the second. One look at the expression in his eyes decided his identity—he would be Thomas.

The model for the next disciple was no problem. In fact, I knew him well. His interest in the project grew as he questioned me about which Apostle he would be.

"Why Matthew, who else?" I responded.

After only a moment's consideration, he replied, "I don't see why not. And, as you know, I am Jewish."

The next step was a good deal tougher. Who would play the part of Judas? I approached a man whose features seemed to conjure up images of Judas in my own mind. A quick "No" was followed by this simple explanation: He wouldn't mind, but the members of the church where he was a minister might! A few months later my wife and I were visiting another city, and there spotted simultaneously a man that we believed should be Judas. Several moments of silence followed my startling request to him. His face then lit up in consent as he said, "Well, Judas must have had his good points—the Apostles made him their treasurer."

Searching through my notes on this Apostle, I stopped short at Matthew 27:3-4. "Then Judas . . . repented . . . saying I have sinned . . . I have betrayed the innocent blood." Remorse rather than treachery is threaded through those verses. And so just before the picture was to be snapped, the model turned his head down and away to achieve this effect.

Not all the model selections were so dramatic. The man who portrayed Philip had been to the studio before when the completion of his masters work called for a commemorative portrait. Yet I can just see him sitting on the Mount of Olives and hanging on to every word of Christ. Or listen to the account of Bartholomew, the fifth disciple to be photographed. I was sitting in a restaurant one day when a truck driver walked in, and I followed him out of the cafe when he finished his cup of coffee. Although a beard already covered his face, he was somewhat hesitant. The next day found him in my studio dressed as Bartholomew, the fifth of the Twelve.

It is also interesting to note the similarities of some of the models' occupations. They aren't fishermen, but two of the men are doctors. The model now known as Andrew is a cardiologist. James the Less is a podiatrist. This James is the only portrait that had to be done over, incidentally. Sometimes growing a good beard takes longer than you think.

You may wonder when the "One" was added to the Chosen Twelve. I awoke early one morning with the idea of a title change—*The Chosen Twelve Plus One.* An intriguing title, and a way to include my favorite of Christ's followers. The person I asked to sit for Paul at first did not feel qualified to step into the sandals of "the least of all apostles." But a subsequent trip to the Holy Land fanned his enthusiasm, and he became the crusading missionary of New Testament times.

What about that crusading spirit known as the unflappable Peter? The model for Peter happens to be a member of my church, and our pastor agreed that his large frame and work-worn hands singled him out particularly for this role. His six-foot, four-inch size cannot be fully appreciated in the picture.

Judas the Thrice-Named or Thaddeus happened to have his office right next door, and he actually enjoyed growing his beard while visiting several Indian reservations to buy jewelry for his store. James did not experience such joy when he altered his appearance due to the nature of his work as a branch bank manager. In fact, had it not been for a local celebration of frontier times called the Gold Rush Days, another model for James would have had to be found.

Someone told me of a barber in a nearby town that might fit the next part. I dropped into his shop one day, and not too long after he came to mine. When I told him I wanted him to pose as the one called the Zealot, a twinkle came into his eyes.

"The old rabble-rouser, huh?" he chuckled. "That sure describes my life before I accepted Christ. Well, Simon the Zealot it is!"

The final one of the Twelve was another visitor from out of town. He'd made the trip to be at his father's funeral. And I saw him outside a lawyer's office, sitting in a car and thumbing through some papers. The thirty-four-year old man could simply not believe that I wanted him to pose as an Apostle.

"Who, me?" he said incredulously. "Wait 'til my wife hears this."

But the sitting wasn't as easy as just going and telling his wife. He lived more than seven hundred miles away. It was January, but he promised to return the following month. February came and went. So did March. And April. Still, no John. Just as I was ready to look for someone else, the "Apostle John" returned! The door of my studio flew open on May 1, and he stuck his head in to ask the sheepish question, "Were you serious about wanting me to pose for you?"

With a shower of reassurance I welcomed him back, this totally disabled Vietnamese war veteran and model for the disciple whom Jesus loved. The Apostle John, then, completed the series, just as he had completed the canon of Scripture two thousand years ago with the writing of the book of Revelation.

There you have it. The stories behind the selection of the men photographed for *The Chosen Twelve Plus One*. They are from different cities. They are involved in different businesses. They each have different interest and talents. Just like the disciples of the Lord.

And they are like the Lord's Chosen in another way, too. They are real people. Just like the disciples were. If you were to take any one of the Apostles out of his time in history and place him in today's clothing and on today's streets, no one would notice him. Hopefully that's what this book has done for you. Conveyed the reality of those men in their time. They were ordinary men bound together by a common need—the need for a Savior. And that is where the parallel of the disciples of long ago with men of today is most crucial. Because we have that same need. The question is, Will we realize that need and become His followers?

Harry A. Hollett

The book is set in Centaur and Arrighi by Mackenzie-Harris Corp., San Francisco. The display face used is Rivoli. Printed by Schultz-Wack-Weir Inc., Portland. Binding by Hiller Industries, Salt Lake City.

*Design by Dannelle Pfeiffer*